MARKE
PROFESSIONALS

PRACTICAL CAREER GUIDES

Series Editor: Kezia Endsley

MARKETING PROFESSIONALS

A Practical Career Guide

KEZIA ENDSLEY

ROWMAN & LITTLEFIELD
Lanham • Boulder • New York • London

Published by Rowman & Littlefield
An imprint of The Rowman & Littlefield Publishing Group, Inc.
4501 Forbes Boulevard, Suite 200, Lanham, Maryland 20706
www.rowman.com

86-90 Paul Street, London EC2A 4NE

British Library Cataloguing in Publication Information Available

Library of Congress Cataloging-in-Publication Data

Names: Endsley, Kezia, 1968– author.
Title: Marketing professionals : a practical career guide / Kezia Endsley.
Description: Lanham : Rowman & Littlefield, [2022] | Series: Practical career guides | Includes bibliographical references. | Summary: "Marketing Professionals: A Practical Career Guide includes interviews with marketing professionals. This book covers the following job areas in marketing: Digital marketing, SEO (search engine optimization) and web analytics, Social media marketing, Graphic design, Brand management, Product marketing"—Provided by publisher.
Identifiers: LCCN 2021025445 (print) | LCCN 2021025446 (ebook) | ISBN 9781538159309 (paperback) | ISBN 9781538159316 (epub)
Subjects: LCSH: Marketing—Vocational guidance.
Classification: LCC HF5415.35 .E53 2022 (print) | LCC HF5415.35 (ebook) | DDC 658.80023—dc23
LC record available at https://lccn.loc.gov/2021025445
LC ebook record available at https://lccn.loc.gov/2021025446

Contents

Introduction

*W*elcome! If you are interested in finding out about careers under the marketing umbrella, you've come to the right book. This book is an ideal place to start if you want to understand the various careers available to you. It discusses the different paths you can follow to ensure you have all the training, education, and experience needed to succeed in your career goals.

There is a lot of good news about this field. Job outlook is good and job satisfaction is high. It's a great career choice for anyone with a desire to make a living using their creativity and people skills in a professional setting.

When considering any career, your goal should be to find your specific nexus of interest, passion, and job demand. Although it is important to consider job outlook and demand, educational requirements, and other such practical

A career in marketing can be creative and fulfilling! ©*nd3000/iStock/Getty Images Plus*

matters, remember that you'll be spending a large portion of your life in whatever career you choose, so you should also find something that you enjoy doing and are passionate about. Of course, it can make the road easier to walk if you choose something that's in demand and pays the bills as well.

A Career in Marketing

A career in marketing can take many, many different paths, depending on what you are actually marketing. Most marketing these days takes place electronically, whether that be on a website or social media site or in an app. This book breaks down the field of marketing into different areas that all have a strong job outlook in the foreseeable future. This book covers the following job areas in marketing:

- Digital marketing and advertising
- Social media marketing
- SEO (search engine optimization) and web analytics
- Graphic design
- Brand management
- Product marketing

This book will discuss these main areas and the day-to-day responsibilities of each.

So what exactly do professionals in marketing do on the job, day in and day out? What kinds of skills and educational background do you need to succeed in this field? How much can you expect to make, and what are the pros and cons of each area? How do you determine if marketing is a good fit for you, and which area best fits your talents and interests? This book can help you answer these questions and more.

For each of these areas of marketing, the book covers the pros and cons, the educational requirements, projected annual wages, personality traits that are well suited, working conditions and expectations, and more. You'll even read some interviews from real professionals working in marketing. The goal is for you to learn enough about marketing in all its iterations to give you a clear view as to which career path is a good fit. And if you still have more questions, this book will also point you to resources where you can learn even more.

The Job Market Today

The US Bureau of Labor Statistics (BLS) is part of the US Department of Labor. Its *Occupational Outlook Handbook* (OOH) tracks statistical information about thousands of careers in the United States. Because the field of marketing is so broad, diverse, and dynamic, it's best to look at several different occupations to get the best overall picture of the market. The OOH includes the following forecasts for jobs similar to or fitting under the marketing umbrella:

- Public relations specialists are expected to experience job growth of about 7 percent between 2019 and 2029, which is faster than the average job growth rate (about 1.4 percent).[1]
- Careers in advertising, promotions, and marketing are expected to enjoy a growth of about 6 percent in the next decade.[2]
- Careers under the marketing research umbrella are expected to grow 18 percent in the next decade.[3]
- Careers under the social media specialist umbrella are expected to grow around 10 percent in the next decade.[4]

Print publishing and the use of print materials continue to shrink as more and more information is presented visually on phones and computer screens. As a result, companies are continuing to increase their digital presence, requiring their employees to help market and curate their content to users. Although employment in newspaper, periodical, book, and directory publishers is projected to decline significantly, job prospects are strong for those who specialize in digital marketing in one format or another.[5]

The bottom line is that your job prospects will be best if you keep up with the latest trends, technologies, and techniques. Chapter 1 covers lots more about the job prospects in these areas and breaks down the numbers in each area into more detail.

What Does This Book Cover?

The goal of this book is to cover all aspects of marketing and explain the differences between the various areas and how you can excel in them. Here's a breakdown of the chapters:

- Chapter 1 explains the different careers under the umbrella of marketing that are covered in this book. You'll learn about what the professionals mentioned in this introduction do in their day-to-day work, the different environments in which marketing professionals work, some pros and cons about each, the average salaries of these jobs, and the outlook for marketing in general.
- Chapter 2 explains the educational requirements of these different areas, from high school diplomas to bachelor's degrees and beyond. You will learn how to go about getting experience (in the form of internships, for example) in these various settings before you enter college as well as during your college years.
- Chapter 3 explains all the aspects of college and postsecondary schooling that you'll want to consider as you move forward. You will learn how to get the best education for the best deal. You will also learn a little about scholarships and financial aid and how the SAT and ACT work.
- Chapter 4 covers all aspects of the résumé-writing and interviewing processes, including creating a dynamic portfolio that conveys your unique style, writing a stellar résumé and cover letter, interviewing to your best potential, dressing for the part, communicating effectively, dealing with stress, and more.

> "If you want to get into this career because you like posting pictures and you think that's fun, that's fine but it won't be enough to sustain a career. Writing and communication skills are critical. You don't have to be an English professor, but you do need to hone your ability to write well, in different ways."—Michelle Freed, social media communications consultant

Where Do You Start?

You can approach the marketing field in a few different ways—whether your interest is in graphic design, social media marketing, brand management, or product marketing, this book can help answer your questions and show you the path to realize your aspirations. In any case, when you work in marketing, you will need to meld the creative and artistic with knowledge of technologies and communication as they change in our evolving digital world!

Your future awaits! ©*Delpixart/iStock/Getty Images Plus*

The good news is that you don't need to know the answers to these questions yet. In order to find the best fit for yourself in marketing, you need to understand how these different career options are structured. That's where you'll start in chapter 1.

Why Choose a Career in Marketing

*Y*ou learned in the introduction that marketing as a career is diverse, strong, and constantly changing and growing. You learned that to have the best prospects for success, you need to learn and keep up with technology as well as learn how to communicate effectively. You also were reminded that it's important to pursue a career that you enjoy, are good at, and are passionate about. You will spend a lot of your life working; it makes sense to find something you enjoy doing. Of course, you want to make money and support yourself while doing it. If you love the idea of being creative for a living but you also enjoy tapping into your analytical side, you've come to the right book.

This chapter breaks out the job areas that typically fall under the marketing umbrella and covers the basics of each. After reading this chapter, you should have a good understanding of several of the areas within marketing and can

The field of marketing involves many aspects of communicating, including collaboration, interpreting data, planning, and design. ©*AlexBrylov/iStock/Getty Images Plus*

then start to determine if one of them is a good fit for you. Let's start with discussing what these folks actually do on the job.

What Do Marketing Professionals Do?

When you think of someone in the marketing field, you may picture a lot of different potential scenarios. You may picture a person working on a laptop, helping to write websites and brochures; someone pushing out targeted social media content for their company; someone working to generate and place stories for products; someone running and interpreting web analytics data to determine who is visiting a website; or even someone managing a brand or a line of products. Marketing professionals do all these things and more!

In addition to the different programs and technologies they use, the work of marketing professionals varies greatly depending on the field in which they work, the purpose of their projects (to sell something, to evoke emotion, to convince, etc.), the media in which they work, and more. That's good news, because it means there are a lot of choices and options in this field. To maximize your career options, you need to make sure you continue to educate yourself about the constant changes in the field. Chapters 2 and 3 cover the educational requirements in more depth.

Recall that this book breaks the marketing field into these jobs:

- Digital marketing and advertising
- Social media marketing
- SEO (search engine optimization) and web analytics
- Graphic design
- Brand management
- Product marketing

Keep in mind that your job could entail one or more (or maybe even all) of the areas mentioned above, depending on the field and the size of the company you work for. Although breaking the field down into these areas provides a convenient way to discuss the different aspects of marketing as they currently exist, keep in mind that you may do a little of all of these in a job titled "marketing professional." So the next sections discuss each of these career areas in more detail.

WHAT QUALITIES DO YOU NEED TO SUCCEED IN MARKETING?

Regardless of whether you're leaning more toward social media, digital advertising, web analysis, brand management, or some mix of all of these, there is a core list of important qualities you'll need to have, or at least sharpen over time:

- *Communication skills:* You need to work as part of a team, be able to convey your ideas articulately, and compromise when needed. This includes verbal and written communication.
- *Flexibility and adaptability:* You must be ready to change gears or give up on an idea that you really like and slaved over if it doesn't work for the company or your client. You always have to be prepared to adopt new practices, update your skill set and knowledge base, keep up with industry best practices, and stay current with the latest technologies and trends.
- *Analytical skills:* You must be able to perceive your work from a consumer or client point of view to ensure that the words convey the intended message.
- *Computer skills:* You will very likely use computer programs or write programming code to do most of your work.
- *Creativity:* You must be able to think creatively to develop original ideas and help them come to life.
- *Concentration:* You must sit at a computer and write or create content for long periods.
- *Thick skin:* You must be able to respond well to criticism and feedback and learn not to take it personally, even when it's your personal vision that's being rejected.
- *Time-management skills:* Workdays can be long, particularly when there are tight deadlines. You'll need to be able to manage your time effectively when a deadline is approaching.[1]

Most of these skills can be refined and polished with experience, education, and hard work, so don't worry if you feel like you're not quite there yet. If a career as a marketing professional is what you want, perseverance is key!

DIGITAL MARKETING AND ADVERTISING

Digital marketing or advertising specialist is a broad title that can mean many different things, depending on where you work. This title can refer to web designers/developers, brand managers, product marketers, marketing experts, and more.

Here are some of the typical responsibilities that digital marketing professionals are tasked with:

- Designing digital media campaigns aligned with business goals (alone or as part of a marketing team)
- Coordinating the creation of digital content (website, blogs, press releases, and podcasts)
- Managing end-to-end digital projects
- Helping to establish the company's web presence to promote brand awareness
- Maintaining a strong online company voice through social media
- Working with marketing, sales, and product development teams to brand consistency
- Suggesting and implementing direct marketing methods to increase profitability
- Staying up-to-date with digital media developments[2]

You will very likely be expected to work well in a team setting, in which you develop ideas and campaigns in conjunction with others, all of whom work on different aspects of a project.

Digital marketing professionals focus on "selling the sizzle," as they say. Their role essentially involves designing, creating, and delivering effective on-line marketing programs that support the company's services and products. The goal may be to increase brand awareness or create a brand image, to identify a target market, to promote company products or services, to drive prospects to conversions (sales), or a combination of these.

You may choose to specialize in certain areas, such as search engine optimization (SEO), paid search (PPC or pay-per-click), display media, social media, or shopping feeds. Or you can have more general digital marketing expertise and can still be referred to as a digital marketing specialist.

Key skills you'll need to be a digital marketing specialist include the following:

- Knowing marketing principles in the key areas of SEO, social media, content marketing, e-mail marketing, and PPC
- Being creative and having good presentation skills
- Knowing how to plan, create, and implement a marketing strategy
- Understanding the key measurement tools available
- Developing a social presence and advocating brands effectively
- Collaborating with others
- Staying current in marketing trends and news[3]

SOCIAL MEDIA MARKETING

Social media marketing specialists communicate with the public through platforms (usually social media apps) that allow users to create and share content online. They run their company's social media accounts, working to build the brand's reputation and ensure it is consistent and positive.

Social media specialists post content—such as images, text, and videos—to generate interest in a topic that relates to the company or its brand. They also follow conversations and interact with the public online. These workers also sometimes collaborate with others to promote their employer's cause; for example, they might work on a team with marketing consultants to publicize an event.

To track the effectiveness of their communication strategies, social media specialists will also set goals and then measure success against those goals by measuring likes, reposts, retweets, and so on.[4]

PERSISTENCE IS TRAINABLE!

When your goal is to enter a creative and competitive field such as social media marketing, SEO, or digital communications of any kind, for that matter, persistence is important to your ultimate success. The good news is that persistence is a skill that you can teach yourself. So how do you become persistent?

- *Know your goals.* It's easier to keep moving if you can see where you're going. Be sure to reevaluate now and then, because people's goals change over time.

- *Keep your goals reachable.* How do you eat an elephant? One bite at a time. Don't frighten yourself with large, distant goals. Instead, focus on the next thing you need to do: turn an assignment in on time, critique a website, create a logo, and so on.

- *Know your priorities.* You already know what your priorities are. Get your schoolwork done. Get your work-work done. Hang with your friends. Call your mom. And learn. (Not necessarily in that order.)

- *Make marketing a priority.* Take time to study the online communication all around you, and be sure to carve out time in your schedule to work on your own ideas.

- *Use positive self-talk.* Don't let your inner voice give you a hard time. We all have a nasty little inner voice that makes us doubt ourselves. Counter that voice by purposely talking to yourself in a supportive and positive way. No, not out loud. Tell yourself, "I'm just going to do this now."

- *Get in the habit of getting in the habit.* Pick a thing and do it. Then pick another thing and do that. Repeat.

- *Notice when you finish.* Pay attention to those special times when you complete a project. Feel proud of yourself. See how nice that is? Noticing how good it feels to finish something helps you be persistent in the future.

- *Have patience.* Creating something from nothing takes patience at every stage. Patience doesn't mean sitting around waiting for opportunities to come to you. Patience means accepting that things take time and that fretting and stressing about things doesn't make them happen any sooner. Patience means accepting that if one opportunity doesn't work out, there is always another one.

- *Have faith in yourself and your work.* Perhaps the most important thing that you'll need is to have faith in yourself. Some people seem to be born confident or talented or both. Others need to develop it over the course of a lifetime. Faith in yourself doesn't mean arrogance, or the assumption that you have nothing new or different to learn. It means an internal confidence in your ability to learn, to imagine, and to create that will carry you during difficult times. It means learning to recognize what is good in your work without relying only on the opinions of others. It also means being confident enough in your abilities to recognize when an idea is not working so that you can either fix it or set it aside and move on to something else.

SEO AND WEB ANALYTICS MARKETING

Web analytics specialists, also known as web analysts or sometimes SEO specialists, determine the costs, benefits, drawbacks, and effectiveness of websites and other online campaigns. In other words, they determine how well a site/campaign is doing what it set out to do by measuring the traffic (the number of visitors) that comes to it.

Web analytics specialists need to be current on all the key measurement tools available and must be installing and using the latest tools as they constantly evolve. But that's not all they do. Because web analytics solutions (such as Google Analytics) run more or less on their own once they're installed, the majority of their job isn't about collecting data but rather *interpreting* it.

On a daily, weekly, monthly, quarterly, or annual basis, web analytics specialists generate and review reports that contain information about visitor demographics and behavior. They then present these reports to company stakeholders such as CEOs, web designers, and other marketing professionals.

For instance, you might be tasked with determining how many people visited your company's website, where those people live, how long they stayed on the site, what and how many web pages they viewed, where on the website they clicked, and what search terms they used to find the website in the first place.[5] All this information is important to your employer/client because it can be used to improve the website so that:

- Visitors stay longer
- Visitors find what they are looking for more easily
- Visitors are encouraged to purchase something, if that's a feature of the site
- Visitors leave the site with a favorable impression of the company
- Information about visitors can be collected (with their permission, of course) to help the company more effectively create marketing campaigns

Web analysis is not typically an entry-level position. As a web analyst, you'll need to be able to interpret web traffic data, visualize data appropriately, understand the dynamics behind a website, be able to integrate market research, and use and understand web analytics tools and interpret the data you get from them. A background or degree in marketing is a good place to start.

GRAPHIC DESIGN

In the most general sense, graphic designers use 2D or 3D art to create visual concepts that inspire, inform, and captivate users. They work on logos and layout designs for magazines, brochures, reports, advertisements, and more. They create designs, but they also have to consider things like negative space, readability, and typography.

Sometimes also called layout artists, they design the structure of text and images in a good-looking format, often for printed forms of media. Other typical positions or titles that graphic designers hold include creative director, art director, art production manager, brand identity developer, and illustrator.[6]

Graphic designers overwhelmingly work in studios, where they have access to equipment such as drafting tables, computers, and software. Although many graphic designers work independently as freelancers, those who work for specialized graphic design firms are often part of a creative team. Many graphic designers collaborate with colleagues or work with clients on projects.

According to the Bureau of Labor Statistics, in 2018 about 20 percent of graphic designers worked for themselves as freelancers, 10 percent worked in specialized design services (such as architectural, engineering, scientific, and other technical fields), 8 percent worked in advertising, public relations, and related services, 7 percent worked in print support, and 5 percent worked for newspaper, periodical, book, and directory publishers.[7]

Graphic designers create projects for their employer or for clients. Some of their responsibilities include the following:

- Planning a visual concept by studying materials and understanding the big picture approach
- Illustrating a concept by creating a rough layout of art and copy; this usually includes the arrangement, size, and style of all elements
- Creating guidelines for how logos and other branding materials should be displayed and used
- Helping to make design choices (e.g., fonts and colors) for all content the company will use
- Preparing final copy and art by operating typesetting, printing, and similar equipment
- Completing projects on time by coordinating with outside agencies, art services, printers, and so on

- Maintaining technical knowledge by attending design workshops, reviewing professional publications, and participating in professional societies
- Working with other creative team members to produce content and get results, as needed[8]

In addition to working well with others on a team, graphic designers need to be creative, flexibile, deadline-oriented, and detail-oriented, and be able to take criticism and handle feedback.

BRAND MANAGEMENT

The job of the brand manager is to ensure that the public perception of the company's brand is consistently conveyed across all platforms. This requires a big-picture view of the company and of the marketing efforts it employs. How the public perceives a certain brand is shaped directly by the efforts of the brand manager.

Brand managers craft an image and promote it to the public. This usually involves a very deep understanding of the brand, its products or services, its positioning in the market, and its target audience.

Brand managers are also typically responsible for overseeing all marketing campaigns, including TV ads, magazine and newspaper ads, events and exhibitions, websites, social media sites, and so on.[9]

Overseeing a brand is an important responsibility, and it requires consistency among all marketing efforts and collaboration with colleagues to stay on the same page. Because it's helpful to have experience with marketing in all respects, customer relationship management skills, and budget management prowess, these jobs are typically not entry-level positions.[10]

PRODUCT MARKETING

Product marketing managers are responsible for many of the same aspects as the brand manager is, but instead of doing this for a whole brand or line of products, they are responsible for one particular product. They are responsible for developing effective marketing strategies for the product in question, and they focus on ensuring that the message about that product is consistent across all the marketing platforms the company employs.

Their duties usually include influencing the pricing and packaging of the product, guiding sales and marketing teams, collaborating with others to develop messaging and market positioning around the product, and gathering and interpreting customer feedback about the product.[11]

The Pros and Cons of the Marketing Field

Keep in mind that the roles described above aren't always separate jobs. In a small company or start-up, marketing professionals may be responsible for some combination of these roles. That means you'll need some technical know-how, some marketing savvy, great communications skills, and a good mix of people and technical skills. Chapter 2 covers the educational expectations in full.

As with any career, one in marketing has upsides and downsides. But also true is that one person's pro is another person's con. If you love working in teams and collaborating with others, then this could well be the right job for you; if you prefer to work solo, it's probably going to be frustrating for you at times. If you like the rush of a hurried deadline, ever-changing specifications, and due dates, and don't mind working long hours at times, then you will get a charge out of marketing!

LEARNING BY "SEEING"

Although it's one thing to read about the pros and cons of a particular career, the best way to really get a feel for what a typical day is like on the job and learn about the challenges and rewards is to talk to someone who is working in the profession.

It's also a good idea to arrange to job shadow with a professional in the field working in whichever capacity you find most interesting. Job shadowing means accompanying someone to work, observing the tasks involved, the work culture, the environment, the hours, and the intensity of the work. Talk with people you know who work in the business to find job shadowing opportunities.

You can also learn a lot by reading the interviews with actual professionals that you find throughout this book.

Although each profession within marketing is different, some generalizations can be made when it comes to what is most challenging and most gratifying about the field.

Some general pros include:

- The work tends to be creative and challenging.
- You'll get paid to spend time on your favorite platforms.
- You can potentially get real-time feedback about how you're doing.
- In this competitive field, you will have colleagues who share your passion and from whom you can learn.
- Your work has the potential to go viral or have a positive impact!
- It is a constantly evolving field with new trends and innovations and endless opportunities for learning.
- There is a vast degree of variety in work environments, from large corporations to start-ups to freelance work from anywhere.
- There is flexibility in terms of the kind of degree you need; you can choose one of several paths to a career in marketing.

Some general cons include:

- The working hours can be long and irregular. You can expect to sometimes work early and late hours and also on weekends in order to meet pressing deadlines or deal with any number of unpredictable issues or situations that may arise.
- Because of the high degree of collaboration, you should expect to have to surrender an idea or even a whole design that you feel attached to. You have to be flexible and think as a team member rather than as an individual creator.
- It is a high-pressure field that requires an ability to manage stress well and to multitask. You need a thick skin in order to be able to handle criticism and feedback.
- You have to constantly evolve to keep your performance up and continue to compete. Advancing to the next level can take a lot of time, hard work, creativity, and patience.

The good news is that you can control some of the above factors. You can eliminate or mitigate many of these drawbacks by carefully choosing the environment you work in. Let's talk more about the job market next.

Collaborating with other smart and creative people who you respect can be one of the great joys of working in marketing. ©*ferrantraite/E+/Getty Images Plus*

"Keeping on top of all the digital trends and making sure your creativity works for social media is important and can be challenging. You have to keep on top of it and keep abreast of the latest technology."—Sue Porritt, graphic designer

How Healthy Is the Job Market?

Recall from the introduction that the Bureau of Labor Statistics, which is part of the US Department of Labor, tracks statistical information about thousands of careers in the United States. Data about careers in digital communications differ greatly depending on the area of focus/approach. Let's look at each area.

DIGITAL MARKETING AND ADVERTISING

This general area of digital marketing includes brand managers and product managers, although, as mentioned, those two positions require more experience and thus command a higher average salary commensurate with experience.

- *Education:* Varies from an associate degree in marketing, public relations, web design, or related field to a bachelor's degree in computer science or programming
- *2020 median income:* $73,760
- *Job outlook 2019–2029:* 8 percent (faster than average)
- *Work environment:* In the computer systems design and related services industry; some people are self-employed and still others work in industries including publishing, management consulting, and advertising[12]

SOCIAL MEDIA MARKETING

- *Education:* Bachelor's degree in marketing, public relations, communications, business, or a related field
- *2020 median income:* $56,700
- *Job outlook 2019–2029:* 6 percent (faster than average)
- *Work environment:* In the computer systems design and related services industry; some people are self-employed and others work in industries including publishing, management consulting, and advertising[13]

SEO AND WEB ANALYTICS

- *Education:* Bachelor's or master's degree in marketing, communications, business, or an information technology–related field
- *2020 median income:* $48,590
- *Job outlook 2019–2029:* 7 to 10 percent (much faster than average)
- *Work environment:* Many are employed in specialized design services, publishing, or advertising, public relations, and related services industries[14]

GRAPHIC DESIGN

- *Education:* Varies from an associate degree in web design or related field to a bachelor's degree in computer science or programming
- *2020 median pay:* $69,430
- *Job outlook 2019–2029:* 13 percent (much faster than average)

- *Work environment:* In the computer systems design and related services industry; some are self-employed and others work in industries including publishing, management consulting, and advertising[15]

Since more and more industries are moving from print to online communications in all forms, it's relevant to note that employment of graphic designers in newspaper, periodical, book, and directory publishers is projected to decline 22 percent from 2019 to 2029. However, employment of graphic designers in computer systems design and related services is projected to grow 24 percent over the same period.[16] You can be sure that you are on the right side of that trend by immersing yourself in online graphic design and digital marketing.

WHAT IS A MEDIAN INCOME?

Throughout your job search, you might hear the term "median income" used. What does it mean? Some people believe it's the same thing as average income, but that's not correct. While the median income and average income might sometimes be similar, they are calculated in different ways.

The true definition of median income is the income at which 50 percent of the workers earns more than that income, and the other half of workers earns less. If this is complicated, think of it this way: Suppose there are five employees in a company, each with varying skills and experience. Here are their salaries:

- $42,500
- $48,250
- $51,600
- $63,120
- $86,325

What is the median income? In this case, the median income is $51,600, because of the five total positions listed, it is in the middle. Two salaries are higher than $51,600, and two are lower.

The average income is simply the total of all salaries divided by the number of total jobs. In this case, the average income is $58,359.

Why does this matter? The median income is a more accurate way to measure the various incomes in a set because it's less likely to be influenced by extremely high or low numbers in the total group of salaries. For example, in our example of five incomes, the highest income ($86,325) is much higher than the other incomes, and therefore it makes the average income ($58,359) much higher than most incomes in the group. Therefore, if you base your income expectations on the average, you'll likely be disappointed to eventually learn that most incomes are below it. But if you look at median income, you'll always know that 50 percent of the people are above it and 50 percent are below it. That way, depending on your level of experience and training, you'll have a better estimate of where you'll end up on the salary spectrum.

MICHELLE FREED: SOCIAL MEDIA COMMUNICATIONS CONSULTANT

Michelle B. Freed. *Courtesy of Michelle B. Freed*

Michelle B. Freed received her bachelor's degree in journalism from the University of Oklahoma with a public relations emphasis. Her initial focus was on PR and corporate communications. She has spent most of her career in nonprofit communications, currently running her communications consultant company called WoodFish.

At this time, she mainly focuses on social media, although she does enjoy working with teams determining messages and helping with content writing and strategy.

Can you explain how you ended up in public relations? What about it interested you?

At the time, I liked marketing and communications. My main goal in journalism is that I loved to write and was a very curious person. I loved learning about other people. I didn't really want to be a reporter, per se. PR seemed like the best fit at the time.

I worked at a PR agency as well as many nonprofits. My job evolved into writing, which I enjoyed the best. I was a person of all trades—designing, producing, and writing. I created newsletters, nonprofit magazines, etc. Computers were crude at that time. I started learning about software as it became available. I taught myself because that was where the direction was going. I learned coding, design, and so on.

I didn't think about social media until many of my clients about ten years ago began wanting help with it. The social media umbrella became something clients really wanted, so I added that to my toolkit. I'm largely self-taught in these areas.

I do online content, social media management, and messaging throughout all mediums (online, mailers, etc.). My career moved to the digital world.

I am mostly self-taught. Social media evolves all the time. You have to be self-motivated and learn constantly. One way I learn is by partnering with digital marketing companies. The analytics and strategy people teach me a lot and I do more of the creative part. They do more behind-the-scenes coding and analysis.

To be successful, you have to have a good base of communication skills and good knowledge of marketing and strategy. You have to constantly learn new things.

What's a "typical" day in your job? What do you do day to day?

I am a freelancer running my own communications consultant company called WoodFish. I have several large companies I work with regularly, and they are often more structured, as well as smaller companies with short-term projects that tend to be more intense for shorter periods of time. You have to adapt to client needs and expectations.

There really is no typical day, although I do structure my week somewhat. Mondays and Fridays involve planning and working with a flexible content calendar. My day-to-day work is accomplished mostly on Mondays and Fridays too. Tuesdays, Wednesdays, and Thursdays are meetings (Zooms) with clients—strategy meetings and setting the tone for the social media message. I meet with every client once a month for social media planning. I am also creating new content and doing research on these days. I always have a buffer built in.

You have to be flexible and be able to rearrange your schedule. Social media by nature changes quickly and trends come up. Flexibility is key! Being able to juggle priorities is important as well.

What is the best part of being in this field?

It's never boring! You have to become a quick expert on a lot of different things, which can be a lot of fun. It can be challenging too. I also enjoy meeting people. You need people skills because you will deal with all different kinds of people.

The flexibility is really nice too. I can work from anywhere. Except for in-person meetings, I can arrange my schedule to work whenever it's best for me. I can be there for my kids when I need to. The constant variety is great. The creative aspect of it is great too.

I am naturally interested in news and current events and pop culture, and all of that comes in handy when you work with social media.

Do you think your education adequately prepared you for your current career path?

As much as it could at the time, I think so. If you want to be in communications of anything, you must be a good writer and a solid communicator. This is true in any profession, really. My roles have naturally evolved, but the key skills of writing and communicating well are very important. It's not about posting neat pictures.

My education taught me the fundamentals of writing, which was important.

What has been most surprising about your career path?

Working in social media is not just sitting around posting. It's much more about strategizing and working with others. You have to make connections and develop relationships. There is a lot of work that goes on behind the scenes—brand development, etc. You have to get information proactively. Social media bleeds into a lot of other things. The best social media managers have experience and can see the big picture and have knowledge of the other pieces.

It is much more time-consuming than you think to create an effective brand and social media presence.

Everybody has access to websites and social media—so everyone is out there making noise. What needs to remain constant are the personal connections with people. Connecting to people emotionally sets you apart. It's fun to have a glossy approach, but you have to be authentic. If you're too fake, people will know or find out and that only damages the brand. Authenticity is key.

Technology will shift and change but knowing how to tell people stories will never be out of fashion.

What traits or skills make for a good digital communications professional?

If you want to be in communications in any field, you must be a good writer and a solid communicator. This is true in any profession, really.

You need to be self-aware in this field too. There are many gray areas here—you must be aware of your own strengths and weaknesses and learn new things. The soft skills and having a high EQ (emotional quotient) are really important to be successful.

Making connections is very important too. You can't do all this on your own, especially when you are a freelancer. Networking is important—you want it to be natural for them to think of you when they have an issue.

You are sometimes in the role of customer service. You need the skills to do that successfully. Flexibility is also important. Having some data analysis skills is also important.

What advice do you have for young people considering this career? How can a young person prepare for this career while in high school?

Of course, stay up on the platforms that businesses use. Try to find a mentor that you can talk to. Making connections is important. Also follow different kinds of accounts that you think are good and see what they are doing.

Social media offers a lot of opportunities for young people to get their foot in the door. Try to get your feet wet at a small company your family knows, so you can start to practice. When you build a little experience, you might find little jobs here and there to help small companies.

If you want to get into this career because you like posting pictures and you think that's fun, that's fine but it won't be enough to sustain a career. Try to get even the most basic experience from a company. Learn as much as you can. Writing and communication skills are critical. You don't have to be an English professor, but hone your ability to write well, in different ways.

Would I Succeed in Marketing?

This is a tough question to answer, because really the answer can only come from you. But don't despair: There are plenty of resources both online and elsewhere that can help you find the answer by guiding you through the types of questions and considerations that will bring you to your conclusion.

Of course, no job is going to match your personality or fit your every desire, especially when you are just starting out. There are, however, some aspects to a job that may be so unappealing or simply mismatched that you may decide to opt for something else, or you may be so drawn to a feature of a job that any downsides are not that important.

Having excellent communication skills and a passion for communications and marketing in all its forms is particularly important in this field, of course.

But there are other factors to keep in mind as well. One way to see if you may be cut out for this career is to ask yourself the following questions:

- *Am I a creative person who is also able to let an idea I may love go because others disagree or it just isn't possible?*
  Any creative person feels attached to their ideas. When you are working alone on your own vision, you have full control over what the end result will be. It doesn't work that way when you work creatively with a team and when you have a client who has a different vision and the ultimate say in how things look.
- *Am I able to follow directions even if I don't agree? Am I able to understand instructions quickly?*
  Working in a team can be a fulfilling and inspiring experience, and this field provides that for the most part. However, it does require being comfortable with others making final decisions and understanding quickly what you are tasked with doing.
- *Can I be creative under tight deadlines?*
  Working under tight deadlines can be exhilarating, but it can also cause you to experience moments of "idea freeze." Can you work through those creative morasses? Are you willing to work some long hours and weekends when needed?
- *When something goes wrong, can I think quickly on my feet to find a solution? Do I have the leadership skills to direct others to problem solve?*
  Because this is a fast-paced industry where everything can change at any time, being flexible and staying calm under pressure are paramount. Equally important is being able to provide solutions or suggestions when something goes awry.

- *Can I consistently deal with people in a professional, friendly way?*
  Communication is a key skill to have in any profession, but particularly as a marketing professional, because it's important to convey clearly and concisely what your expectations and visions are.

If the answer to any of these questions is an adamant *no*, you might want to consider a different path. Remember that learning what you *don't* like can be just as important as figuring out what you *do* like to do.

Are you ready for a creative and rewarding career in marketing? ©*Chinnapong/iStock/Getty Images Plus*

If you pursue a career that fundamentally conflicts with the person you are, you won't be good at it and you won't be happy. Don't make that mistake. If you need help determining your key personality factors, take a career-counseling questionnaire to find out more. You can find many online or ask your school guidance counselor for reputable sources.

Summary

In this chapter, you learned a lot about the different types of careers that exist under the general marketing umbrella. You've learned about what social media marketing professionals do in comparison with product marketing managers, for example. You also learned about some pros and cons of this field, the median salaries of these jobs, and the outlook in the future for various areas of marketing. You hopefully even contemplated some questions about whether your personal likes and preferences meld well with this career. Are you starting to get excited about the idea of working in marketing? If not, that's okay, as there's still time.

Chapter 2 dives into forming a plan for your future, covering everything there is to know about educational requirements, internship opportunities, and more, about each of these areas of marketing. You'll learn about finding summer jobs and learn how to start building a portfolio that has your own unique sensibility as well. The goal is for you to set yourself apart—and above—the rest.

2

Forming a Career Plan in Marketing

*I*t's not easy to choose a career, yet it's one of the most important decisions you will make in your life. There are simply so many options available, and it is easy to feel overwhelmed. Particularly if you have many passions and interests, it can be hard to narrow your options down. That you are reading this book means you have decided to investigate a career in marketing, which means you have already discovered a passion for communications, technology, and on-going learning. But even within this industry, there are many choices, including what role you want to pursue, what work environment you desire, and what type of work schedule best fits your lifestyle.

Now that you have some idea about the different career opportunities under the marketing umbrella, it's time to formulate a career plan. For you organized folks out there, this can be a helpful and energizing process. If you're not a naturally organized person, or perhaps the idea of looking ahead and building a plan to adulthood scares you, you are not alone. That's what this chapter is for.

After we talk about ways to develop a career plan (there is more than one way to do this!), the chapter dives into the various educational requirements. Finally, it looks at how you can gain experience through school activities such as the high school yearbook, Twitter account, or newspaper; job shadowing; volunteering; part-time jobs; and more. Yes, experience will look good on your résumé, and in some cases it's even required, but even more important, getting out there and working in marketing in various settings is the best way to determine if it's really something that you enjoy. When you find a career that you truly enjoy and have a passion for, it will rarely feel like work at all.

If you still aren't sure if the marketing field is right for you, try a self-assessment questionnaire or a career aptitude test. There are many good ones on the web. As an example, the career resource website Monster.com includes free self-assessment tools at www.monster.com/career-advice/article

/best-free-career-assessment-tools. The Princeton Review also has a very good aptitude test geared toward high schoolers at www.princetonreview.com/quiz /career-quiz.

YOUR PASSIONS, ABILITIES, AND INTERESTS: IN JOB FORM!

Think about how you've done at school and how things have worked out at any temporary or part-time jobs you've had so far. What are you really good at, in your opinion? What have other people told you you're good at? What are you not very good at right now, but you would like to become better at? What are you not very good at, and you're okay with not getting better at?

Now forget about work for a minute. In fact, forget about needing to ever have a job again. You won the lottery—congratulations! Now answer these questions: What are your three favorite ways to spend your time? For each one of those things, can you describe why you think you are particularly attracted to it? If you could get up tomorrow and do anything you wanted all day long, what would it be? These questions can be fun, but can also lead you to your true passions. The next step is to find the job that sparks your passions.

Your ultimate goal should be to match your personal interests, goals, and aptitude with your preparation plan for college and career. Practice articulating your plans and goals to others. When you feel comfortable speaking about your aspirations, that means you have a good grasp of your goals and your plan to reach them.

Tip: Marketing professionals have reported having associate and bachelor's degrees in marketing, business, communications, advertising, journalism, public relations, multimedia studies, and even in creative writing. The exact degree is not as important as showing you can earn a degree and having the initiative and desire to pursue a career in marketing.[1]

Planning the Plan

The following are things to think about deeply when planning your career path.

- *Think about your interests outside of the work context.* How do you like to spend your free time? What inspires you? What kind of people do you like to surround yourself with? How do you best learn? What do you really love doing?
- *Brainstorm a list of the various career choices under the marketing umbrella that you are interested in pursuing.* Organize the list in order of which careers you find most appealing, and then list what it is about each that attracts you. This can be anything from work environment to geographical location, to the type of communications, to the specific role you desire.
- *Research each job on your career choices list.* You can find job descriptions, salary indications, career outlook, salary, and educational requirements information online, for example.
- *Consider your personality traits.* How do you respond to stress and pressure? Do you consider yourself a strong communicator? Do you work well in teams or prefer to work independently? Do you consider yourself creative? How do you respond to criticism? It is important to keep these in mind to ensure you choose a career path that makes you happy and in which you can thrive.
- *Although your choice of career is obviously a huge factor in your future, it's important to consider what other factors feature in your vision of your ideal life.* Think about how your career will fit in with the rest of your life, including whether you want to live in a big city or small town, how much flexibility you want in your schedule, how much autonomy you want in your work, what your work environment should be like, and what your ultimate career goal is.
- *While there are lucrative careers in the marketing field, many job opportunities that offer experience to newcomers and recent graduates can come with relatively low salaries.* What are your pay expectations, now and in the future?

Thinking deeply about these questions and answering them honestly will help make your career goals clearer and guide you in knowing which steps you will need to take to get there.

You are on a fact-finding mission of sorts. A career fact-finding plan, no matter what the field, should include these main steps:

- Find out about educational requirements and schooling expectations. Will you be able to meet any rigorous requirements? This chapter will help you understand the educational paths.
- Seek out opportunities to volunteer or shadow someone doing the job. This will enable you to experience in person what the atmosphere is like, what a typical workday entails, how coworkers interact with each other and with management, and whether you can see yourself thriving in that role and work culture. Use your critical-thinking skills to ask questions and consider whether this is the right environment for you.
- Look into student aid, grants, scholarships, and other ways you can get help to pay for schooling.
- Build a timetable for taking required exams such as the SAT and ACT, applying to schools, visiting schools, and making your decision. You should write down all the important deadlines and have them at the ready when you need them.
- Continue to look for employment that matters during your college years—internships and work experiences that help you get hands-on experience and knowledge about your intended career.
- Talk with professionals working in the job you are considering and ask them what they enjoy about their work, what they find the most challenging, and what path they followed to get there.
- Find a mentor in the field who is interested in helping you. This person can be a great source of information, education, and connections. Don't expect a job (at least not at first); just build a relationship with someone who wants to pass along his or her wisdom and experience. Coffee meetings or even e-mails are a great way to start.

A mentor can help you in many ways. ©*Kerkez/iStock/Getty Images Plus*

Where to Go for Help

If you aren't sure where to start, your local library, school library, and guidance counselor's office are great places to begin. Search your local or school library for resources about finding a career path and finding the right schooling that fits your needs and budget. Make an appointment with or e-mail a counselor to ask about taking career interest questionnaires. With a little prodding, you'll be directed to lots of good information online and elsewhere. You can start your research with these five sites:

- The Bureau of Labor Statistics' Career Outlook site at www.bls.gov /careeroutlook/home.htm. The US Department of Labor's Bureau of Labor Statistics site doesn't just track job statistics, as you learned in chapter 1. An entire section of the BLS website is dedicated to helping young adults looking to uncover their interests and to match those interests with jobs currently in the market. Check out the section called "Career Planning for High Schoolers." Information is updated based on career trends and jobs in demand, so you'll get practical information as well.

- The Mapping Your Future site at www.mappingyourfuture.org. This site helps you determine a career path and then helps you map out a plan to reach those goals. It includes tips on preparing for college, paying for college, job hunting, résumé writing, and more.

- The Education Planner site at www.educationplanner.org. With separate sections for students, parents, and counselors, this site breaks down the task of planning your career goals into simple, easy-to-understand steps. You can find personality assessments, get tips on preparing for school, read Q&As from counselors, download and use a planner worksheet, read about how to finance your education, and more.
- The TeenLife site at www.teenlife.com. Calling itself "the leading source for college preparation," this site includes lots of information about summer programs, gap year programs, community service, and more. Promoting the belief that spending time out "in the world" outside of the classroom can help students do better in school, find a better fit in terms of career, and even interview better with colleges, this site contains lots of links to volunteer and summer programs.
- Educations.com provides a career test designed to help you find the job of your dreams at www.educations.com/career-test.

Use these sites as jumping-off points and don't be afraid to reach out to real people, such as a guidance counselor or your favorite teacher, for more assistance.

The process of deciding on and planning a career path is daunting. In many ways, the range of choices of careers available today is a wonderful thing. It allows us to refine our career goals and customize them to our own lives and personalities. In other ways, though, too much choice can be extremely daunting and require a lot of soul-searching to navigate clearly.

Tip: Young adults with disabilities can face additional challenges when planning a career path. DO-IT (Disabilities, Opportunities, Internetworking, and Technology) is an organization dedicated to promoting career and education inclusion for everyone. Its website (https://www.washington.edu/doit/) contains a wealth of information and tools to help all young people plan a career path, including self-assessment tests and career exploration questionnaires.

ERIK DAFFORN: SEO ANALYTICS CONSULTANT

Erik Dafforn. *Courtesy of Erik Dafforn*

Erik Dafforn earned his bachelor's degree in English from Wabash College. He currently works as a search engine optimization (SEO) and analytics consultant. This means he helps clients build and maintain websites that people can find through search engines, and he helps companies understand all the traffic coming to their sites.

After working for an online marketing company for about fifteen years, he started his own company about six years ago. It is a one-person organization, and he enjoys the freedom this offers, because delegating work has always been difficult for him. In his current role, he does all the work, and he gets either all the credit or all the blame for a project. He's okay with that.

Can you explain how you ended up in this field? What about it interested you? Is it what you expected it would be?

I landed in the internet marketing industry by accident. With an English degree, I started out in book publishing. After a few publishing jobs, I was working as a part-time contractor with an internet marketing company writing web page content, analysis documents, and press releases. I was intrigued by what the SEO team was doing, because it seemed very mysterious but also very cool. This was before Google had a significant presence in the industry, so the engines we really focused on were AltaVista, Yahoo!, HotBot, Lycos, and other engines a lot of people don't remember.

I learned SEO from people who had been around at its very beginning. There were no published rules or guidelines—much like the entire internet was at that time. Today, there is a vast body of work out there about how to make your site perform well for search engines, and I was able to take part in writing some of that.

What's a "typical" day in your job?

In any given day, I do a variety of things:

- Build traffic reports or presentations for clients that show an analysis of their web traffic numbers and other usage statistics (online sales, time spent on site, and so on).

- Make recommendations about how clients should change or build their websites. This includes explaining why I've made those recommendations and predicting what the results of those changes or actions will be.
- Use some of my tools to perform research into user behavior. This might be a keyword research tool, which describes how people use search engines to find information. It might also be a user-experience (UX) tool, which shows how people interact with web pages—where they click, how far they scroll down the page, and so on.
- Meet with other teams or workers that work on the same projects I do. That might be the marketing team, programmers, or supervisors for a particular website.
- Because I'm self-employed, I also do a lot of things that aren't directly in the crosshairs of my discipline:
    - Build and send invoices and contracts to clients
    - Prepare sales pitches and presentations

What's the greatest challenge the market faces at this time? What are your greatest challenges, day in and day out?

As an external consultant (someone who doesn't work full-time for any particular company), I face several challenges, and they all revolve around consistently being able to prove that I'm worth the money I charge to clients.

Many companies want to bring all their marketing resources "in house," which means they want to minimize the number of external contactors they use. Being an external contractor, it's up to me to show them that keeping me is a good deal for them. So it's not enough to simply help them when they have a problem; instead, I often need to identify their problems before they do and present a solution.

There is always a lot of new technology to keep track of. I get to see the most current techniques in web development, and it's my job to make sure those techniques still enable Google, for example, to properly interpret the content. So I spend a lot of time looking at code, crawling through a site like Google does, and making educated guesses about how a site redesign or code changes will affect a client's marketing numbers.

What's the best part of being in this field?

I really enjoy the clients that I work with. I enjoy helping them succeed and watching their businesses grow. I get to learn more about the industries that my clients are in, such as higher education, construction, property management, retail, and tourism.

I enjoy spending time with really smart people, and my clients are just that. They come from different backgrounds and different countries, but the common thread among them is their desire to do good work and succeed at their jobs.

What's the most challenging part of being in this field?

Search engines like Google are constantly innovating and modifying their code with the goal of ensuring that their users have a good experience on the site. This is important, but it can be hard to keep track of all the different features they offer and to know which ones are important and worth my clients' time. When my clients ask about a particular feature or search engine recommendation, I need to make sure I've not only heard about it, but that I have an opinion on it before they ask. Keeping up with all the documentation can be a challenge.

Do you think your education adequately prepared you for your current job?

I do. Even though I was an English major, the foundation of my education consisted of doing research, building an argument or position, then using a narrative (either written or a spoken presentation) to describe and defend that claim. Today, much of what I do uses that same approach.

Where do you see this field going in the future?

People will always use technology to search for information, ask questions, and make transactions. The challenge will be to keep up with the different ways they do those things. Twenty years ago, this involved sitting at a large computer and typing search queries over and over until you found results that helped you. Today, people can buy things directly from a phone or ask a question to their smart speaker. Making sure your content is formatted for all these various methods of interaction—and that you can measure that interaction—will always be essential skills.

What traits or skills make for a good SEO/marketing manager?

I think the best SEO and marketing managers understand that while SEO is important, it's only one piece in a larger puzzle. This is a lesson that a lot of SEO workers have learned over time. If you build a website focused only on ensuring people *arrive* at the site, chances are the site won't contain a very fulfilling user experience once the visitors arrive.

Therefore, you need to build a site that attracts users, but one that presents a very intuitive interface, easy access to information, and a pathway for the user to take the steps that are logical for her to complete her journey. This means using technology to ensure a fast-loading site, using design features that ensure the user finds the site appealing, and integrating UX features that make it easy and rewarding for the user to stick around on the site for a while.

And finally, you need to be able to measure your results accurately. It's not enough to say that a thousand people visited your site. Which visitors were more engaged with the content? Were site visitors on a phone more valuable than those

on a desktop machine? Which methods of drawing in visitors were the most effective and which could be dropped?

What advice do you have for young people considering this career?
I think SEO and web marketing in general are good careers to consider because
they touch so many other career types: web development, programming, brand
management, e-commerce, advertising, and general marketing. You'll interact with
smart people with a variety of skills, and you'll come away with a really broad
understanding of how electronic communication plays out.

How can a young person prepare for this career while in high school?
Build a website. (Make sure the site is an extension of your own passions or hob-
bies, or else you won't enjoy it!) Install analytics and watch your traffic closely. How
are visitors finding you? What can you do to increase your traffic or improve the
user experience? And how can you prove, through data, that your changes resulted
in better numbers? Those are all essential characteristics of a web marketer, and
performing experiments in traffic generation—and being able to document and
present them—will help you create an excellent portfolio.

═══════════════

Making High School Count

Regardless of the career you choose, there are some basic yet important things
you can do while in high school to position yourself in the most advantageous
way. Remember—it's not just about having the best application, it's also about
figuring out which areas of marketing you actually would enjoy and which ones
don't suit you.

- Hone your communication skills in English, speech, and debate. You'll
  need excellent communication skills in a job where you'll have to speak
  with everyone from coworkers to clients to bosses.
- Take classes in marketing and advertising.
- Become comfortable using all kinds of computer software and digital
  tools such as Google Analytics.

- Volunteer in as many settings as you can. Read on to learn more about this important aspect of career planning.
- Take online courses in HTML, JavaScript, the Adobe suite (Photoshop, Illustrator, InDesign, and Acrobat), and so on. You can find relatively inexpensive courses online and gain access to expensive software at a reduced student rate (or use the versions at your high school).

Courses to Take in High School

Depending on your high school and what courses you have access to, there are many subjects that will help you prepare for a career in marketing. If you go to a school that offers marketing, journalism, creative writing, or multimedia courses, those are good places to start. However, there are other courses and subjects that are just as relevant. Some of them may seem unrelated initially, but they will all help you prepare yourself and develop key skills.

- *Language arts.* Because team collaboration is the essence of a job in the marketing industry, ensuring you know how to communicate clearly and effectively—both in spoken and written language—will be key. It helps avoid unnecessary frustration, delays, financial and time costs, and errors if you can clearly convey and understand ideas.
- *Interpersonal communication/public speaking.* These courses will be an asset in any profession, including the marketing field. If you need to present ideas or results to your team, to sales staff, to clients, these will be very important skills to hone.
- *Business and economics.* As with any type of business, if you have the ambition to run your own, knowledge gained in business and economics classes will prepare you to make smarter business and financial decisions.
- *Specialized software.* Marketing professionals need to be skilled in the technical tools they use daily in their work. This could include tools as diverse as HTML, JavaScript, Google Analytics, and the Adobe suite, as well as multimedia apps and programs.

Gaining Work Experience

The best way to learn anything is to do it. When it comes to preparing for a career in marketing, there are several options for gaining real-world experience and getting a feel for whether you are choosing the right career for you.

The one big benefit of jobs in the marketing field is you don't have to land a work-experience opportunity at an established or upcoming company to prove what you've got and what you can do. Rather than wait for someone to invite you to work for them, you are wise to keep working on your own, to show not only your talent but also your passion.

This means you should get out there and create a podcast with your friend about your favorite pastime, for example, or create a mock social media campaign for a favorite website or brand, or create some of your own websites and build a strong portfolio. Be sure to create works that are suitable to the market you want to get into.

Educational Requirements

Depending on the type of job you want to pursue in marketing, various levels of education are required. In fact, as you read earlier, there are many different degrees that can lead to a rewarding career in marketing.

In some cases, it is possible to enter the field without a college degree—but in order to advance to higher levels in your career, a degree is usually preferred by employers. The general requirements in terms of education for all marketing jobs are similar. A bachelor's degree or an associate degree in marketing or advertising, business, public relations, communications, journalism, web design, or a related field are common ways that people begin careers as marketing professionals.

> "Good marketers pick up nuances in customer conversations and behaviors and turn those into competitive advantages. Communication is important in all areas of business, but especially in marketing. Communication—both written and verbal—is critical, and you must be able to do both well."—Melisa Duffy, marketing director

This chapter discusses the considerations to keep in mind when deciding what level of education is best for you to pursue. Chapter 3 will outline in more detail the types of programs offered.

WHY CHOOSE AN ASSOCIATE DEGREE?

With a two-year degree—called an associate degree—you are qualified to apply for certain positions within marketing. Common associate degrees offered that pertain to marketing are in entry-level marketing (of course), advertising, business, web design, public relations, and communications.

These degree programs are sufficient to give you a knowledge base to begin your career, and can serve as a basis should you decide to pursue a four-year degree later. Do keep in mind, though, that many jobs within the marketing field are quite competitive. With so much competition out there, the more of an edge you can give yourself, the better your chances will be.

Keep in mind that community colleges and technical schools can be a much cheaper way (as much as half the cost) to earn the same degree, and as long as the program is accredited, it won't always matter to potential employers that you didn't attend a more well-known university.

WHY CHOOSE A BACHELOR'S DEGREE?

A bachelor's degree—which usually takes four years to obtain—is a requirement for most careers related to the marketing industry. In general, the higher education you pursue, the better your odds are to advance in your career, which means more opportunity and often better compensation.

The difference between an associate and a bachelor's degree is, of course, the amount of time each takes to complete. To earn a bachelor's degree, a candidate must complete forty college credits, compared with twenty for an associate degree. This translates to more courses completed and a deeper exploration of degree content, even though similar content is covered in both.

In addition to deciding how long you should go to school, another important conclusion to come to is whether you consider yourself a creative person who will learn the programs and applications needed to be creative or a technical person who wants to use technology to create things and be creative. This isn't a subtle difference when it comes to the career trajectory. It could mean the difference between a marketing degree and a computer science degree, both of which can end in the field of marketing!

The bottom line? Keep in mind also that once you have a few years' related experience under your belt, employers rarely care or even look to see what your original degree was. They won't ask about your education; they just want to know what kind of experience you have.

Also, no matter the path you choose, make sure the university or college you attend is properly accredited so that your degree will mean something to employers out in the real world.

The type of degree you decide to pursue is dependent on many factors, including your educational goals, your career plans, and your budget. Remember: there is no one right answer. ©*dragana991 /iStock/Getty Images Plus*

WHAT'S THE DIFFERENCE BETWEEN ACCREDITATION AND CERTIFICATION?

The terms *accreditation* and *certification* can be confusing, and people often mix them up and use them incorrectly, contributing to the overall confusion. Accreditation is the act of officially recognizing an organizational body, person, or educational facility as having a particular status or being qualified to perform a particular activity; for example, schools and colleges are accredited.

Certification, on the other hand, is the process of confirming that a person has certain skills or knowledge. This is usually provided by some third-party review, assessment, or educational body. Individuals, not organizations, are certified. This also might be referred to as being licensed. Certification programs are generally available through software product vendors, such as Google. Such certifications can give you a competitive advantage over your peers.

Experience-Related Requirements

There are many ways you can gain helpful experience in the marketing field before and during the time you're pursuing your education. This can and should start in high school, especially during the summers. Experience is important for many reasons:

- Shadowing others in the profession can help reveal what the job is really like and whether it's something that you think you want to do, day in and day out. This is a relatively risk-free way to explore different career paths. Ask any seasoned adult and they will tell you that figuring out what you *don't* want to do is sometimes more important than figuring out what you *do* want to do.
- Internships and volunteer work are a relatively quick way to gain work experience and develop job skills.
- Volunteering can help you learn the intricacies of the profession, such as what types of environments are best and which skills you need to work on.

- Gaining experience during your high school years sets you apart from the many others who are applying to postsecondary programs.
- Volunteering in the field means that you'll be meeting many others doing the job that you might someday want to do (think: career networking). You have the potential to develop mentor relationships, cultivate future job prospects, and get to know people who can recommend you for later positions.

Consider these tidbits of advice to maximize your volunteer experience. They will help you stand out:

- *Get diverse experiences.* For example, try to shadow in at least two different places of business.
- *Try to gain forty hours of volunteer experience in each setting.* This is typically considered enough to show that you understand what a full work week looks like in that setting. This can be as few as four to five hours per week over ten weeks or so.
- *Don't be afraid to ask questions.* Just be considerate of others' time and wait until they are not busy to pursue your questions. Asking good questions shows that you have a real curiosity about the profession.
- *Maintain and cultivate professional relationships.* Write thank-you notes, send updates about your application progress and tell them where you decide to go to school, and check in occasionally. If you want to find a good mentor, you need to be a gracious and willing mentee.[2]

Look at these kinds of experiences as ways to learn about the profession, show people how capable you are, and make connections with others that could last throughout your career. It may even help you to get into the college of your choice, and it will definitely help you write your personal statement that explains why you want to work in marketing.

Another way to find a position—or at least a company that is open to curious students—is to start with their website and visit the websites listed in this book. Also, don't be afraid to just pick up the phone and call local companies. Be prepared to start by making copies, assisting with clerical work, and other such tasks. Being on-site, no matter what you're doing, will teach you more than you know. With a great attitude and work ethic, you will likely be given more responsibility over time.

Networking

Because it's so important, a last word about networking: It's important to develop mentor relationships even at this stage. Remember that about 85 percent of jobs are found through personal contacts.[3] If you know someone in the field, don't hesitate to reach out. Be patient and polite, but ask for help, perspective, and guidance.

Making connections with others in your prospective field is a great way to learn and be exposed to opportunity. ©*skynesher/E+/Getty Images Plus*

If you don't know anyone, ask your school guidance counselor to help you make connections. Or pick up the phone yourself. Reaching out with a genuine interest in knowledge and a real curiosity about the field will go a long way. You don't need a job or an internship just yet—just a connection that could blossom into a mentoring relationship. Follow these important but simple rules for the best results when networking:

- Do your homework about a potential contact, connection, university, school, or employer before you make contact. Be sure to have a general understanding of what they do and why. But don't be a know-it-all. Be open and ready to ask good questions.
- Be considerate of professionals' time and resources. Think about what they can get from you in return for mentoring or helping you.
- Speak and write using proper English. Proofread all your letters, e-mails, and even texts. Think about how you will be perceived at all times.
- Always stay positive.
- Show your passion for the subject matter.

Summary

In this chapter, you learned about some ways to figure out whether marketing is the right field for you. This chapter discussed the educational options for the different areas of marketing. You also learned about getting experience and job shadowing. At this time, you should have a good idea of the schooling options and the paths you might consider taking. You hopefully even contemplated some questions about what kind of educational path fits your strengths, time requirements, and wallet. Are you starting to picture your career plan? If not, that's okay, as there's still time.

Remember that no matter which of these areas you pursue, you must maintain your knowledge of the latest and greatest computer programs, tools, and applications used in your field. Advances in technology are frequent and constant, and it's vitally important that you keep apprised of what's happening in your field. The bottom line is that you need to have a lifelong love of learning to succeed in any digital field, and that includes marketing.

Chapter 3 goes into a lot more detail about pursuing the best educational path. The chapter covers how to find the best value for your education and includes discussion about financial aid and scholarships. At the end of chapter 3, you should have a clearer view of the educational landscape and how and where you fit in.

Pursuing the Education Path

*W*hen it comes time to start looking at colleges, universities, or postsec-ondary schools, many high schoolers tend to freeze up at the enormity of the job ahead of them. This chapter will help break down this process for you so it won't seem so daunting.

Yes, finding the right college or learning institution is important, and it's a big step toward achieving your career goals and dreams. The last chapter covered the various educational requirements of careers in the marketing field, which means you should now be ready to find the right institution of learning. This isn't always just about finding the very best school that you can afford and are accepted into, although that might end up being your path. It should also

It's important to find a postsecondary school that fits your needs and budget. ©*martin-dm/E+/Getty Images Plus*

be about finding the right fit so that you can have the best possible experience during your post–high school years.

But the truth is that attending postsecondary schooling isn't just about getting a degree. It's also about learning how to be an adult, managing your life and your responsibilities, being exposed to new experiences, growing as a person, and otherwise moving toward becoming an adult who contributes to society. College—in whatever form it takes for you—offers you an opportunity to become an interesting person with perspective on the world and empathy and consideration for people other than yourself, if you let it.

An important component of how successful you will be in college is finding the right fit, the right school that brings out the best in you and challenges you at different levels. I know—no pressure, right? Just as with finding the right profession, your ultimate goal should be to match your personal interests, goals, and personality with the college's goals and perspective. For example, small liberal arts colleges have a much different feel and philosophy than Big 10 or PAC-12 state schools. And rest assured that all this advice applies even if you're planning on attending community college or another postsecondary school.

Don't worry, though: In addition to these soft skills, this chapter does dive into the nitty-gritty of how to find the best fit, no matter what you want to do.

WHAT IS A GAP YEAR?

Taking a year off between high school and college, often called a gap year, is normal, perfectly acceptable, and almost required in many countries around the world. It is becoming increasingly acceptable in the United States as well. Even Malia Obama, President Obama's daughter, did it. Because the cost of college has gone up dramatically, it literally pays for you to know going in what you want to study, and a gap year—well spent—can do lots to help you answer that question.

Some great ways to spend your gap year include joining organizations such as the Peace Corps or AmeriCorps, enrolling in a mountaineering program or other gap year–styled program, backpacking across Europe or other countries on the cheap (be safe and bring a friend), finding a volunteer organization that furthers a cause you believe in or that complements your career aspirations, joining a Road Scholar program (see www.roadscholar.org), teach English in another country (more information is

available at www.gooverseas.com/blog/best-countries-for-seniors-to-teach-english
-abroad for more information), or working and earning money for college!

Many students will find that they get much more out of college when they have a year to mature and to experience the real world. The American Gap Year Association reports from alumni surveys that students who take gap years show greater civic engagement, higher college graduation rates, and higher grade point averages (GPAs) in college.[1] You can use your gap year to explore and solidify your thoughts and plans about a career in marketing, as well as add impressive experiences to your college application. See the association's website at https://gapyearassociation.org for lots of advice and resources if you're considering this potentially life-altering experience.

Finding the College That's Right for You

Before looking into which schools have the degrees you're interested in, it will behoove you to take some time to consider what type of school will be best for you. Answering questions like the ones that follow can help you narrow your search and focus on a smaller set of choices. Write your answers to these questions down somewhere where you can refer to them often, such as in the Notes app on your phone:

- *Size*: Does the size of the school matter to you? Colleges and universities range in size from five hundred or fewer students to twenty-five thousand students.
- *Community location:* Would you prefer to be in a rural area, a small town, a suburban area, or a large city? How important is the location of the school in the larger world?
- *Distance from home:* Will you live at home to save money? If not, how far away from home—in terms of hours or miles away—do you want or are you willing to go?
- *Housing options:* What kind of housing would you prefer? Dorms, off-campus apartments, and private homes are all common options.
- *Student body:* How would you like the student body to look? Think about coed versus all-male and all-female settings, as well as ethnic and

racial diversity, how many students are part-time versus full-time, and the percentage of commuter students. Who will you likely meet there?

- *Academic environment:* Which majors are offered, and at which degree levels? Research the student-faculty ratio. Are the classes taught often by actual professors or more often by the teaching assistants? How many internships does the school typically provide to students. Are independent study or study abroad programs available in your area of interest?
- *Financial aid availability/cost:* Does the school provide ample opportunities for scholarships, grants, work-study programs, and the like? Does cost play a role in your options? (For most people, it does.)
- *Support services:* How strong are the school's academic and career placement counseling services?
- *Social activities and athletics:* Does the school offer clubs that you are interested in? Which sports are offered? Are scholarships available?
- *Specialized programs:* Does the school offer honors programs or programs for veterans or students with disabilities or special needs?

"Knowledge is indivisible. When people grow wise in one direction, they are sure to make it easier for themselves to grow wise in other directions as well. On the other hand, when they split up knowledge, concentrate on their own field, and scorn and ignore other fields, they grow less wise—even in their own field."—Isaac Asimov[2]

Not all of these questions are going to be important to you, and that's fine. Be sure to make note of aspects that don't matter as much to you. You might change your mind as you visit colleges, but it's important to make note of where you are to begin with.

Consider the School's Reputation

One factor in choosing a college or certificate program is the school's reputation. This reputation is based on the quality of education previous students have had there. If you go to a school with a healthy reputation in your field, it gives potential employers a place to start when they are considering your credentials and qualifications.

Factors vary depending on which schools offer the program you want, so take these somewhat lightly. Some of the factors affecting reputation generally include:

- *Nonprofit or for-profit.* In general, schools that are nonprofit (or not-for-profit) organizations have better reputations than for-profit schools. In fact, it's best to avoid for-profit schools.
- *Accreditation.* Your program must be accredited by a regional accrediting body to be taken seriously in the professional world. It would be very rare to find an unaccredited college or university with a good reputation.
- *Acceptance rate.* Schools that accept a very high percentage of applicants can have lower reputations than those that accept a smaller percentage. That's because a high acceptance rate can indicate that there isn't much competition for those spaces, or that standards are not as high.
- *Alumni.* What have graduates of the program gone on to do? The college's or department's website can give you an idea of what their graduates are doing.
- *History.* Schools that have been around a long time tend to be doing something right. They also tend to have good alumni networks, which can help you when you're looking for a job or a mentor.
- *Faculty.* Schools with a high percentage of permanent faculty compared to adjunct faculty tend to have better reputations. Bear in mind that if you're going to a specialized program or certification program, this might be reversed—these programs are frequently taught by experts who are working in the field.
- *Departments.* A department at one school might have a better reputation than a similar department at a school that's more highly ranked overall. If the department you'll be attending is well known and respected, that could be more important than the overall reputation of the institution itself.

There are a lot of websites that claim to have the "Top 10 Schools" for this and that. It's hard to tell which of those are truly accurate. So where do you begin? *U.S. News & World Report* is a great place to start to find a college or university with a great reputation. Go to www.usnews.com/education to find links to the highest-ranked schools for the undergraduate or graduate degree programs you're interested in.

CHRIS SHUTE: CREATIVE DIRECTOR AND BRANDING EXPERT

Chris Shute. *Courtesy of Chris Shute*

Chris Shute started his creative education at Herron Art School during his senior year of high school. During that time, he built his portfolio to get into postsecondary art school. He went to a traditional college for two years, then moved to the Art Academy of Cincinnati and earned a BFA in marketing and advertising.

His first job was in Nashville, Tennessee, in country music entertainment promotions (from T-shirt design to albums to concert poster design); it included NASCAR marketing and advertising design. He spent two years there.

He then moved back to Indiana and became a marketing director for a direct-mail marketing firm, where he spent four years there before deciding he wanted to work for a traditional ad agency.

He worked for small to medium-sized ad firms. This included campaign writing, advertising, and headline writing. It was the media of the day—outdoor, print ads, TV commercials, and radio. He got bigger and bigger clients, including medical device branding and design as well as national brands and companies.

He started at his current job in 1998. He works at a small firm, so he can directly interface with clients and create and nurture relationships directly. He likes having more control over the clients and their expectations.

Can you explain how you became interested in graphic design?

I loved drawing and art as a kid. I don't think of myself as a true fine artist, but I loved telling stories using pictures. I loved getting pads of paper for gifts and just kept drawing. I also loved coming up with stories. Fiction, horror, and comedy, it didn't matter—I loved telling stories with pictures. Even in grade school, I did ads. I saw TV ads and thought I could do better.

Advertising was just something I gravitated to. I had a talent for it. I could draw and could put ideas on paper that others would respond to. I had good rapport with art teachers and I won some contests here and there. It all kept growing my confidence in my ability. In fact, I still draw and enjoy working in pencil. I love Western art and like drawing images that evoke strong emotion.

Can you talk about your current position? What is your title? What do you do day to day?

Creative director is my title. A small agency doesn't really have titles, but that would be it. It's all encompassing and big picture. The understanding and knowing what to ask, when to listen, when to be quiet, and when to advise. Understanding the product/service or objective and then setting the tone with messaging or imaging. Then I direct all the players needed to actually execute the process—videographers, photographers, writers, web developers, artists, printers, TV stations, and so on. I am the owner of it and make sure it's all in line and consistent with what the client wants. I also pitch the idea at the beginning.

The art director brings the creative director's big ideas and vision to life. The creative director is more concerned about the big picture.

I enjoy helping companies brand and rebrand themselves. I like to help a small company that's had a lot of success figure out how to fine-tune their brand after they have outgrown their original concept. This encompasses design, collateral, website content, and beyond. You build a good story. Storytelling is important with branding. Taking a company that's outgrown their brand and bringing them forward to the new concept is challenging but also really enjoyable.

What's the best part of being a graphic designer?

Being able to do what I like and am good at and make a living. This is my natural talent. This is all I enjoyed. A true affinity and ability for the job can lead to good rewards—more money, your ideas are fun to see come to life, and collaboration with other people is rewarding.

It takes collaboration and communication to make a good idea a great one. If everyone wants to make it better, the idea will grow and get better. If it's only personal opinion, it's a difficult process. You have to be open-minded and know that a great idea can come from anywhere but is made better by a team. I enjoy that collaboration.

What is the hardest part of your job and why?

Working with a client that doesn't understand what we do and might not value what we do is challenging. They have unrealistic expectations, so you might spend a lot of your time convincing them about what they need. If they aren't open to real change, it's an uphill battle. They think they want it, but then pull back and don't let marketing reach the potential that you know it could.

When you are starting off, there's a lot of uncertainty—where do you start, where are there jobs, how can you get your foot in the door, will your ideas get accepted, are you good enough, are you as good as your peers. It's pretty competitive and can be cutthroat. People's egos get in the way.

What are some things in this profession that are especially challenging right now?

Longevity is difficult in this business. You need real perseverance to break in and succeed. You can lose your enthusiasm. You have to stay in it to succeed.

Finding clients that value what you do and are willing to pay for it to do it well. Budgets are always a problem. Finding the right budgets for the projects and cost expectations. Marketing is often the first thing that companies cut when things are bad. Companies have found ways to do more with less since the recession—especially with small to midsize companies.

What are some characteristics of a good graphic designer?

Having a thick skin is important. Being a good listener and understanding that the client isn't "wrong." You have to see the other side of the coin. Clients know all about their products, of course, but they often don't know why people want them. A good design will find their audience and the benefit, and then create a story so the audience says, "Ah ha, I need that." A good designer will design to that. It's all about the buyer/client and who they are selling to. If they have that in their mind, it works.

What advice do you have for young people considering this career?

Have perseverance, stay tough, and hang in there. It's not a sprint—you are in it for the long haul. If you hone your skills and continue to grow and understand what it takes to succeed, you'll do well. You have to continually do it—live it, breathe it, etc. You have to be dedicated to it.

Strive for better work and don't get your feelings in it. Learn to take criticism. Be tough. Some of it's very valuable and you need to be open-minded to hear it. Critique in art is a hard thing—you have to build up your skin.

How can a young person prepare for a career in graphic design while in high school?

Take all the art classes that you can. Also, creative writing, radio station, and TV production classes if you can. Understanding psychology is also important for marketing skills. Try to get into a company to shadow or intern, even just to make copies. Get in so you hear the lingo and see how the profession really works. If you have code development, you can help update code, use WordPress, and so on.

Any last thoughts?

Web development, social media, app development, and digital tools in general are all key components of web design. I look at them as tools in the toolbox. Digital media is one of the biggest tools today. Understanding how online ads work, learning how a website's user interface works, and being able to create apps that make it fun to engage with a product are all key components.

A website is a tool; social media is a tool. You must understand them in a broad sense to know what they provide to your client.

It's not an easy field. It's competitive and tight. You have to stick with it, hone your skills, and sell yourself and your ideas. Learn how to stand up in front of people. Learn how to be comfortable in front of a crowd and speak with conviction. If you waffle, your clients will sense that and they will waffle too. But it has to be real.

After the Research, Trust Your Gut

U.S. News & World Report puts it best when it reports that the college that fits you best is one that:

- Offers a degree that matches your interests and needs
- Provides a style of instruction that matches the way you like to learn
- Provides a level of academic rigor to match your aptitude and preparation
- Offers a community that feels like home to you
- Values you for what you do well[3]

Tip: According to the National Center for Education Statistics (NCES), which is part of the US Department of Education, six years after entering college for an undergraduate degree, only 60 percent of students have graduated.[4] Barely half of those students will graduate from college in their lifetime.[5]

By the same token, it's never been more important to get your degree. College graduates with a bachelor's degree typically earn 66 percent more than those with only a high school diploma and are also far less likely to face unemployment. Also, over the course of a lifetime, the average worker with a bachelor's degree will earn approximately $1 million more than a worker without a postsecondary education.[6]

As you look at the facts and figures, you also need to think about a less quantifiable aspect of choosing a college or university: *fit*. What does that mean? It's hard to describe, but students know it when they feel it. It means finding not only the school that offers the program you want but also the school that feels right. Many students have no idea what they're looking for in a school until they walk onto the campus for a visit. Suddenly, they say to themselves, "This is the one!"

Touring the campus and talking to current students are really important. ©*SDI Productions/E+/Getty Images Plus*

While you're evaluating a particular institution's offerings with your conscious mind, your unconscious mind is also at work, gathering information about all kinds of things at lightning speed. When it tells your conscious mind what it's decided, we call that a gut reaction. Pay attention to your gut reactions! There's good information in there.

Hopefully, this section has impressed upon you the importance of finding the right college fit. Take some time to paint a mental picture about the kind of university or school setting that will best meet your needs.

Tip: According to the US Department of Education,[7] as many as 32 percent of college students transfer colleges during the course of their educational career.[8] This is to say that the decision you initially make is not set in stone. Do your best to make a good choice, but remember that you can change your mind, your major, and even your campus. Many students do it and go on to have great experiences and earn great degrees.

Honing Your Degree Plan

This section outlines the different approaches you can take to get a degree that will land you your dream job in marketing, whether it be in web analytics, graphic design, digital marketing, brand management, product marketing, or something else altogether.

Relevant Degree Paths to Consider

As you've no doubt learned after reading this far into the book, the marketing umbrella has many varied but related professions within it. No matter which area you want to focus on, having at least an associate degree (a two-year degree) will give you a leg up during the interviewing process. The good news is that your degree can be in a variety of areas—including marketing (of course), advertising, business, journalism, graphic design, and public relations! Consider these points:

- As an associate degree is a two-year process, it's cheaper and takes less time. Some marketing professionals start their careers with associate degrees in an entry-level position. Once you are hired, your employer may pay for you to get your bachelor's degree.
- If you want to enter the workforce in web analytics or doing data interpretation and visualization, you'll likely need a bachelor's degree (a four-year degree). This could be in computer or information science, communications, business, marketing, or advertising.

So what does the typical marketing degree require? Well, as a sampling, the typical business/marketing student usually takes the following classes:

- Business-to-business (B2B) marketing
- Marketing research and analysis
- Marketing strategy and management
- Internet marketing and advertising
- Brand marketing
- E-commerce

A typical computer design degree will offer courses on the following subjects:

- Introduction to computer graphics
- Computer animation
- Digital modeling
- Graphic design
- 3D design

A typical digital communications/journalism degree will offer courses on the following subjects:

- Digital media arts
- Corporate communication/public relations
- Feature writing
- Creative writing
- Digital animation
- Information systems management

These are just samples of classes you will take to earn a degree. Be sure to check the curricula of the schools you're considering attending for more specific information. The point is that you can choose among several different majors if you want a career in marketing.

Starting Your College Search

If you're currently in high school and you are serious about working in the marketing field, start by finding four to five schools in a realistic location (for you) that offer the degree you're interested in. Not every school near you or that you have an initial interest in will offer the degree you desire, so narrow your choices accordingly. With that said, consider attending a public university in your resident state, if possible; this will save you lots of money. Private institutions don't typically discount resident student tuition costs.

Be sure you research the basic GPA and SAT or ACT requirements of each school as well.

Tip: For students applying to associate degree programs or greater, most advisers recommend taking both the ACT and the SAT during the spring of their junior year. (The ACT is generally considered more heavily weighted in science, so take that into consideration.) You can retake these tests and use your highest score, so be sure to leave time for a retake early in you senior year if needed. You want your best score to be available to all the schools you're applying to by January of your senior year, which will also enable your score to be considered with any scholarship applications. (Unless you want to do early decision, which can provide you certain benefits.) Keep in mind these are general timelines—be sure to check the exact deadlines and calendars of the schools to which you're applying! See the section entitled "Know the Deadlines" for more information about various deadlines.

Once you have found four to five schools in a realistic location for you that offer the degree you want to pursue, spend some time on their websites studying the requirements for admissions. Most universities will list the average stats for the last class accepted to each program. Important factors in your decision about what schools to apply to should include whether or not you meet the requirements, your chances of getting in (but shoot high!), tuition costs, and availability of scholarships and grants, location, and the school's reputation and licensure/graduation rates.

The importance of these characteristics will depend on your grades and test scores, your financial resources, and other personal factors. You will want to find a university with a good degree program that also matches your academic rigor and practical needs.

Choosing a Major

Chapter 2 discussed in some detail the different majors you could pursue if you want to work in the marketing field. There are many, and it basically depends on what field you're interested in. A bachelor's degree in marketing, advertising, or a related field is a great option. However, some people choose a more general degree, such as in business or communications, which may provide you with a more well-rounded education. Others tend toward journalism or something more creative, like graphic design. The good news is that there are many degree paths you can take to end up with a career in marketing. It all depends on your interests and the degrees that appeal most to you, as well as the path that your university provides for marketing degrees.

Regardless of the field of study you choose, you'll need strong communication skills to succeed.

CREATING A PORTFOLIO

Whether or not you need to create a portfolio depends on the area of marketing you want to focus on. If your focus is on content creation, writing, or any other creative aspect of marketing, it might not be a bad idea to build a portfolio of your work.

Your portfolio should showcase all of your best work. At different times in your life, it will contain different types of work depending on what you're using it for. If you are applying to school, your portfolio should be a broad representation of your best work in the various media you use.

So what should your portfolio contain? Different schools will have some different requirements, but in general you want to showcase:

- Ten to twenty examples of your absolute best work—think of your portfolio as your greatest hits
- Variety—showcase the different media you work in
- Personal work—pieces that come from your life or experiences in a way that's meaningful to you
- Your most original work—show your ideas and what you will bring to the experience

- Anything else a specific school has asked you to include, such as your sketchbook[9]

Your portfolio should mostly consist of finished work. Make sure your site is clean and easy to navigate. Don't make people dig through the site to find your work.

Applying and Getting Admitted

Once you've narrowed down your list of potential schools, of course you'll want to be accepted. But first, you need to apply.

There isn't enough room in this book to include everything you need to know about applying to colleges. But here is some useful information to get you started. Remember, every college or university is unique, so be sure to be in touch with the admissions offices of the schools you are interested in so you don't miss any special requirements or deadlines.

Before you go to college, you have to be admitted. ©*Feodora Chiosea/iStock/Getty Images Plus*

Applying to Colleges

It's a good idea to make yourself a to-do list while you're a junior in high school. Already a senior or already graduated? No problem. It's never too late to start.

MAKE THE MOST OF SCHOOL VISITS

If it's at all practical and feasible, you should visit the schools you're considering. To get a real feel for any college or school, you need to walk around the campus and buildings, spend some time in the common areas where students hang out, and sit in on a few classes. You can also sign up for campus tours, which are typically given by current students. This is another good way to see the school and ask questions of someone who knows. Be sure to visit the specific school/building that covers your intended major as well. Websites and brochures won't be able to convey that intangible feeling you'll get from a visit. (If you can't get to a school, see if it offers virtual tours online. Many more schools are providing in-depth campus, dorm, and building tours, especially due to COVID-19.)

Make a list of questions that are important to you before you visit. In addition to the questions listed earlier in this chapter, consider these questions as well:

- What is the makeup of the current freshman class? Is the campus diverse?
- What is the meal plan like? What are the food options?
- Where do most of the students hang out between classes? (Be sure to visit this area.)
- How long does it take to walk from one end of the campus to the other?
- What types of transportation are available for students? Does campus security provide escorts to cars, dorms, and other on-campus destinations at night?

In order to be ready for your visit and make the most of it, consider these tips and words of advice:

- Be sure to do some research. At the very least, spend some time on the college's website. You may find your questions are addressed adequately there.
- Make a list of questions.
- Arrange to meet with a professor in your area of interest or to visit the specific school.

- Be prepared to answer questions about yourself and why you are interested in this school.
- Dress in neat, clean, and casual clothes. Avoid overly wrinkled clothing or anything with stains.
- Listen and take notes.
- Don't interrupt.
- Be positive and energetic.
- Make eye contact when someone speaks directly to you.
- Ask questions.
- Thank people for their time.

Finally, be sure to send thank-you notes or e-mails after the visit is over. Remind recipients when you visited the campus and thank them for their time.

STANDARDIZED TESTS

Many colleges and universities require scores from standardized tests that are supposed to measure your readiness for college and your ability to succeed. There is debate about how accurate these tests are, so some institutions don't ask for them anymore. But most still do, so you should expect to take them.

Undergraduate-Level Tests

To apply to an undergraduate program, students generally take either the SAT or the ACT. Both cover reading, writing, and math. Both have optional essays. Both are accepted by colleges and universities. Both take nearly the same amount of time to complete. If one test is preferred over another by schools, it's usually more about where you live than about the test.[10]

- *SAT:* There are twenty SAT subject tests that you can take to show knowledge of special areas, such as Math 1 and Math 2, Biology (Ecological or Molecular), Chemistry, Physics, US or World History, and numerous languages.

- *ACT:* There aren't any subject tests available with the ACT. Questions are a little easier on the ACT but you don't have as much time to answer them.

Ultimately, which test you take comes down to personal preference. Many students choose to take both exams.

Graduate-Level Tests

- *Graduate Record Exam (GRE), published by Educational Testing Service.* The GRE is the most widely used admission test for graduate and professional schools. It covers verbal and quantitative reasoning and analytical writing. The test results are considered along with your undergraduate record for admissions decisions to most graduate programs.
- *GRE Subject Tests.* Some graduate programs also want to see scores from subject tests. GRE subject tests are offered in biology, chemistry, literature in English, mathematics, physics, and psychology.
- *Medical College Admission Test (MCAT), administered by the Association of American Medical Colleges.* MCAT is the standardized test for admission to medical school programs in allopathic, osteopathic, podiatric, or veterinary medicine (although some veterinary programs accept the GRE instead).
- *Law School Admission Test (LSAT), administered by the Law School Admission Council.* The LSAT is the only test accepted for admission purposes by all American Bar Association–accredited law schools and Canadian common-law law schools.

Know the Deadlines

There are several different acceptance deadlines, with different benefits and timelines:

- *Early decision (ED)* deadlines are usually in November, with acceptance decisions announced in December. Note that if you apply for ED admission and are accepted, that decision is binding, so only apply ED if you know exactly which school you want to go to and are ready to commit.

- *ED II* is a second round of early decision admissions. Not every school that does ED also has an ED II. For those that do, deadlines are usually in January, with decisions announced in February.
- *Regular decision* deadlines can be as early as January 1 but can go later. Decision announcements usually come out between mid-March and early April.
- *Rolling admission* is used by some schools. Applications are accepted at any time and decisions are announced on a regular schedule. Once the incoming class is full, admissions for that year close.

The Common App

The Common Application is a single, detailed application form that is accepted by more than nine hundred colleges and universities in the United States. Instead of filling out a different application for every school you want to apply to, you fill out one form and have it sent to all the schools you're interested in. The Common App itself is free, and most schools don't charge for submitting it.

If you don't want to use the Common App for some reason, most colleges will also let you apply using a form on their website. There are a few institutions that require you to apply through their sites and other highly regarded institutions that only accept the Common App. Be sure you know what is preferred by the schools that interest you.

The Common App website (https://www.commonapp.org) has a lot of useful information, including tips for first-time applicants and for transfer students.

Essays

Part of many college applications is a written essay, and sometimes even two or three. Some colleges provide writing prompts they want you to address. The

Common App has numerous prompts that you can choose from. Here are some issues to consider when writing your essays:

- *Topic.* Choose something that has some meaning for you and that you can speak to in a personal way. This is your chance to show the college or university who you are as an individual. It doesn't have to be about an achievement or success, and it shouldn't be your whole life story. Perhaps choose a topic that relates to a time you learned something or had an insight into yourself.
- *Timing.* Start working on your essays the summer before senior year, if possible. You won't have a lot of other homework in your way, and you'll have time to prepare thoughtful comments and polish your final essay.
- *Length.* Aim for between 250 and 650 words. The Common App leans toward the long end of that range, while individual colleges might lean toward the shorter end.
- *Writing.* Use straightforward language. Don't turn in your first draft—work on your essay and improve it as you go. Ask someone else to read it and tell you what they think. Ask your English teacher to look at it and make suggestions. Do *not* let someone else write any portion of your essay. It needs to be *your* ideas and *your* writing in order to represent *you*.
- *Proofreading.* Make sure your essay doesn't have any obvious errors. Run spell check, but don't trust it to find everything (spell checkers are notorious for introducing weird errors). Have someone you trust read it over for you and note spelling, grammar, and other mistakes. Nobody can proofread their own work and find every mistake—what you'll see is what you expect to see. Even professional editors need other people to proofread their writing! So don't be embarrassed to ask for help.

Letters of Recommendation

Most college applications ask for letters of recommendation from people who know you well and can speak to what you're like as a student and as a person.

How many you need varies from school to school, so check with the admissions office website to see what they want. Some schools don't want any!

WHO SHOULD YOU ASK FOR A LETTER?

Some schools will tell you pretty specifically who they want to hear from. Others leave it up to you. Choose people who know you and think well of you, such as:

- One or two teachers of your best academic subjects (English, math, science, social studies, etc.)
- Teacher of your best elective subject (art, music, media, etc.)
- Adviser for a club you're active in
- School counselor
- School principal (but only if he or she knows you individually as a student)
- Community member you've worked with, such as a scout leader, volunteer group leader, or religious leader
- Boss at a job you've held

WHEN SHOULD YOU ASK FOR A LETTER?

Don't wait until applications are due. Give people plenty of time to prepare a good recommendation letter for you. If possible, ask for these letters in late spring or early summer of your junior year.

SUBMITTING YOUR LETTERS OF RECOMMENDATION

Technically, you're not supposed to read your recommendation letters. This lets recommenders speak more freely about you. Some might show you the letter anyway, but that's up to them. Don't ask to see it!

Recommenders can submit their letters electronically either directly to the institutions you're applying to or through the Common App. Your job is to be sure they know the submission deadlines well in advance so they can send in the letters on time.

Admissions Requirements

Each college or university has its own admissions requirements. In addition, the specific program or major you want to go into may have admissions requirements of its own in addition to the institution's requirements.

It's your responsibility to go to each institution's website and be sure you know and understand the requirements. That includes checking out each department site, too, to find any special prerequisites or other things that they're looking for.

THE MOST PERSONAL OF PERSONAL STATEMENTS

The personal statement you include with your application to college is extremely important, especially if your GPA and SAT/ACT scores are on the border of what is typically accepted. Write something that is thoughtful and conveys your understanding of the program you are interested in, as well as your desire to work in the marketing field. Why are you uniquely qualified? Why are you a good fit for this university and program? These essays should be highly personal (the "personal" in personal statement). Will the admissions professionals who read it—along with hundreds of others—come away with a snapshot of who you really are and what you are passionate about?

Look online for some examples of good ones, which will give you a feel for what works. Be sure to check your specific school for length guidelines, format requirements, and any other guidelines they expect you to follow. Most important, make sure your passion for your potential career comes through—although make sure it is also genuine.

And of course, be sure to proofread it several times and ask a professional (such as your school writing center or your local library services) to proofread it as well.

What's It Going to Cost You?

So, the bottom line: what will your education end up costing you? Of course, this depends on many factors, including the type and length of degree you pursue, where you attend (in-state or not, private or public institution), how much in scholarships or financial aid you're able to obtain, your family or personal income, and many other factors.

> "College may seem expensive. But the truth is that most students pay less than their college's sticker price, or published price, thanks to financial aid. So instead of looking at the published price, concentrate on your net price—the real price you'll pay for a college. . . . Your net price is a college's sticker price for tuition and fees minus the grants, scholarships, and education tax benefits you receive. The net price you pay for a particular college is specific to you because it's based on your personal circumstances and the college's financial aid policies."—BigFuture[11]

The College Entrance Examination Board tracks and summarizes financial data from colleges and universities all over the United States. (You can find more information at www.collegeboard.org.) A sample of the most recent data is shown in table 3.1. It represents the state of things for the 2020–2021 academic year. (It's worth noting that these numbers represent a 2.5 percent increase over 2019–2020 costs before adjusting for inflation.) Costs shown are for one year.

Table 3.1.   Average Estimated Full-Time Undergraduate Budgets (Enrollment-Weighted) by Sector, 2020–2021

	Tuition and Fees	Room and Board	Books and Supplies	Transportation	Other Expenses	Total
Private Nonprofit Four-Year On-Campus	$37,650	$13,120	$1,240	$1,060	$1,810	$54,880
Public Four-Year Out-of-State On-Campus	$27,020	$11,620	$1,240	$1,230	$2,170	$43,280
Public Four-Year In-State On-Campus	$10,560	$11,620	$1,240	$1,230	$2,170	$26,820
Public Two-Year In-District Commuter	$3,770	$9,080	$1,460	$1,840	$2,400	$18,550

NOTES: Expense categories are based on institutional budgets for students as reported in the College Board's Annual Survey of Colleges. Figures for tuition and fees and room and board mirror those reported in Table 1. Books and supplies may include the cost of a personal computer used for study. Other expense categories are the average amounts allotted in determining the total cost of attendance and do not necessarily reflect actual student expenditures.

Keep in mind that these are averages and reflect the published prices, not the net prices. As an example of net cost, in 2019–2020, full-time in-state students at public four-year colleges must cover an average of about $15,400 in tuition and fees and room and board after grant aid and tax benefits, in addition to paying for books and supplies and other living expenses.[12]

If you read data about a particular university or find averages in your particular area of interest, you should assume those numbers are closer to reality than these averages, as they are more specific. These data help to show you the ballpark figures.

Generally speaking, there is about a 3 percent annual increase in tuition and associated costs to attend college. In other words, if you are expecting to attend college two years after these data were collected, you need to add approximately 6 percent to these numbers (assuming there is no global pandemic, which slowed price growth and saw college tuition going down for the first time in one hundred years). Keep in mind this also assumes no financial aid or scholarships of any kind (so it's not the net cost).

The next sections discuss finding the most affordable path to get the degree you want. Later in this chapter, you'll also learn how to prime the pumps and get as much money for college as you can.

Financial Aid and Student Loans

Finding the money to attend college—whether a two- or four-year college program, an online program, or a vocational career college—can seem overwhelming. But you can do it if you have a plan before you actually start applying to college.

NOT ALL FINANCIAL AID IS CREATED EQUAL

Educational institutions tend to define financial aid as any scholarship, grant, loan, or paid employment that assists students in paying their college expenses. Notice that financial aid includes both *money you have to pay back* and *money you don't have to pay back*. That's a big difference!

DO NOT HAVE TO BE REPAID

- Scholarships
- Grants
- Work-study

FUNDS THAT HAVE TO BE REPAID *WITH INTEREST*

- Federal government loans
- Private loans
- Institutional loans

If you get into your top-choice university, don't let the sticker price turn you away. Financial aid can come from many different sources and it's available to cover all the different kinds of costs you'll encounter during your years in college, including tuition, fees, books, housing, and food.

Paying for college can take a creative mix of grants, scholarships, and loans, but you can find your way with some help! ©*Andranik Hakobyan/iStock/Getty Images Plus*

The good news is that universities more often offer incentive or tuition discount aid to encourage students to attend. The market is often more competitive in the favor of the student, and colleges and universities are responding by offering more generous aid packages to a wider range of students than they used to. Here are some basic tips and pointers about the financial aid process:

- You apply for financial aid during your senior year. You must fill out the Free Application for Federal Student Aid (FAFSA) form, which can be filed starting October 1 of your senior year until June of the year you graduate.[13] Because the amount of available aid is limited, it's best to apply as soon as you possibly can. See https://studentaid.ed.gov/sa/fafsa to get started.
- Be sure to compare and contrast deals you get at different schools. There is room to negotiate with universities. The first offer for aid may not be the best you'll get.
- Wait until you receive all offers from your top schools and then use this information to negotiate with your top choice to see if they will match or beat the best aid package you received.
- To be eligible to keep and maintain your financial aid package, you must meet certain grade/GPA requirements. Be sure you are very clear on these academic expectations and keep up with them.
- You must reapply for federal aid every year.

Tip: Watch out for scholarship scams! You should never be asked to pay to submit the FAFSA form ("free" is in its name) or be required to pay a lot to find appropriate aid and scholarships. These are free services. If an organization promises you'll get aid or that you have to "act now or miss out," these are both warning signs of a less-than-reputable organization.

Also, be careful with your personal information to avoid identity theft as well. Simple things like closing and exiting your browser after visiting sites where you entered personal information goes a long way. Don't share your student aid ID number with anyone, either.

It's important to understand the different forms of financial aid that are available to you. That way, you'll know how to apply for different kinds and get the best financial aid package that fits your needs and strengths. The two main categories that financial aid falls under is gift aid, which doesn't have to be repaid, and self-help aid, which includes both loans that must be repaid and work-study funds that are earned. The next sections cover the various types of financial aid that fit into one of these areas.

GRANTS

Grants typically are awarded to students who have financial needs but can also be used in the areas of athletics, academics, demographics, veteran support, and special talents. They do not have to be paid back. Grants can come from federal agencies, state agencies, specific universities, and private organizations. Most federal and state grants are based on financial need. Examples of grants are the Pell Grant and the SMART Grant.

SCHOLARSHIPS

Scholarships are merit-based aid that does not have to be paid back. They are typically awarded based on academic excellence or some other special talent, such as music or art. Scholarships also fall under the areas of athletic-based, minority-based, aid for women, and so forth. These are typically not awarded by federal or state governments but instead come from the specific school you applied to as well as from private and nonprofit organizations.

Be sure to reach out directly to the financial aid officers of the schools you want to attend. These people are great contacts that can lead you to many more sources of scholarships and financial aid. Visit www.gocollege.com /financial-aid/scholarships/types for lots more information about how scholarships in general work.

LOANS

Many types of loans are available especially to students to pay for their postsecondary education. However, the important thing to remember here is that loans must be paid back, with interest. Be sure you understand the interest rate you will be charged. This is the extra cost of borrowing the money and is usually a percentage of the amount you borrow. Is this fixed or will it change over time? Is the loan and interest deferred until you graduate (meaning you don't have to begin paying it off until after you graduate)? Is the loan subsidized (meaning the federal government pays the interest until you graduate)? These are all points you need to be clear about before you sign on the dotted line.

There are many types of loans offered to students, including need-based loans, non-need-based loans, state loans, and private loans. One example of a reputable federal loan is the Direct Stafford Loan. For more information about student loans, start at https://bigfuture.collegeboard.org/pay-for-college/loans /types-of-college-loans.

FEDERAL WORK-STUDY

The US federal work-study program provides part-time jobs for undergraduate and graduate students with financial need so they can earn money to pay for educational expenses. The focus of such work is on community service and work related to a student's course of study. Not all schools participate in this program, so be sure to check with the school financial aid office if this is something you are counting on. The sooner you apply, the more likely you are to get the job you desire and be able to benefit from the program, as funds are limited. See https://studentaid.ed.gov/sa/types/work-study for more information about this opportunity.

FINANCIAL AID TIPS

- Some colleges/universities will offer tuition discounts to encourage students to attend—so tuition costs can be lower than they first appear.
- Apply for financial aid during your senior year of high school. The sooner you apply, the better your chances.
- Compare offers from different schools. One school may be able to match or improve on another school's financial aid offer.
- Keep your grades up. A good GPA helps a lot when it comes to merit scholarships and grants.

- You have to reapply for financial aid every year, so you'll be filling out that FAFSA form again!
- Look for ways that loans might be deferred or forgiven. Service commitment programs are a way to use service to pay back loans.

While You're in College

Once you're in an undergrad program, of course you will take all the classes required by your major. This will be time consuming and a lot of hard work, as it should be. But there's more to your college experience than that!

One of the great advantages of college is that it's so much more than just training for a particular career. It's your opportunity to become a broader, deeper person. Use your electives to take courses far outside your major. Join clubs, intramural teams, improv groups—whatever catches your interest. Take a foreign language. The broader your worldview is, the more interesting you are as a person—and the more appealing you are to employers in the future!

Working While You Learn

Your classes won't always convey what it's like to do the work in real life, especially in the constantly changing world of marketing. If you have the opportunity, consider some of these ways to learn and work at the same time.

COOPERATIVE EDUCATION PROGRAMS

Cooperative education (co-op) programs are a structured way to alternate classroom instruction with on-the-job experience. There are co-op programs for all kinds of jobs. Co-op programs are run by the educational institution in partnership with several employers. Students usually alternate semesters in school with semesters at work.

A co-op program is not an internship. Students in co-op jobs typically work forty hours a week during their work semesters and are paid a regular salary. Participating in a co-op program means it will take longer to graduate, but you'll come out of school with a lot of legitimate work experience.

Be sure the college you attend is truly committed to its co-op program. Some schools are deeply committed to the idea of co-ops as integral to education, but others treat it more like an add-on program. Also, the company you co-op with is not obliged to hire you at the end of the program, but can still be an excellent source of good references for you in your job search.

INTERNSHIPS

Internships are another way to gain work experience while you're in school. Internships are offered by employers and usually last one semester or one summer. You might work part-time or full-time, but you're usually paid in experience and college credit rather than money. There are paid internships in some fields, but they aren't common.

Making High School Count

If you are still in high school, there are many things you can do now to nurture your interest in marketing and set yourself up for success. Consider these tips for your remaining years:

- Work on listening well and speaking and communicating clearly. Work on writing clearly and effectively.
- Learn how to learn. This means keeping an open mind, asking questions, asking for help when you need it, taking good notes, and doing your homework.
- Plan a daily homework schedule and keep up with it. Have a consistent, quiet place to study.
- Talk about your career interests with friends, family, and counselors. They may have connections with people in your community who you can shadow or who will mentor you.
- Try new interests and activities, especially during your first two years of high school.

- Be involved in extracurricular activities that truly interest you and say something about who you are and who you want to be.

Kids are under so much pressure these days to do it all, but you should think about working smarter rather than harder. If you are involved in things you enjoy, your educational load won't seem like such a burden. Be sure to take time for self-care, such as sleep, unscheduled down time, and other activities that you find fun and energizing. See chapter 4 for more ways to relieve and avoid stress.

Remember to take care of yourself and to enjoy the journey to adulthood! ©*AntonioGuillem/iStock /Getty Images Plus*

Summary

This chapter looked at all the aspects of college and postsecondary schooling that you'll want to consider as you move forward. Remember that finding the right fit is especially important, as it increases the chances that you'll stay in school and finish your degree or program—and have an amazing experience while you're there.

In this chapter, you learned a little about the kinds of classes you might take if you want a career in marketing. You also learned about how to get the best education for the best deal. You learned a little about scholarships and financial aid, how the SAT and ACT work, how to write a unique personal statement that eloquently expresses your passions, and how to do your best at essays and other application requirements.

Use this chapter as a jumping-off point to dig deeper into your particular area of interest, but don't forget these important points:

- Take the SAT and ACT early in your junior year so you have time to take them again if you need to. Most schools automatically accept the highest scores, but be sure to check your specific schools' policies.
- Don't underestimate the importance of school visits, especially in the pursuit of the right academic fit. Come prepared to ask questions not addressed on the school website or in the literature.
- Your personal statements/essays are very important pieces of your application that can set you apart from others. Take the time and energy needed to make them unique and compelling.
- Don't assume you can't afford a school based on the sticker price. Many schools offer great scholarships and aid to qualified students. It doesn't hurt to apply. This advice especially applies to minorities, veterans, and students with disabilities.
- Don't lose sight of the fact that it's important to pursue a career that you enjoy, are good at, and are passionate about! You'll be a happier person if you do so.

"It has always seemed strange to me that in our endless discussions about education so little stress is laid on the pleasure of becoming an educated person, the enormous interest it adds to life. To be able to be caught up into the world of thought—that is to be educated."—Edith Hamilton[14]

At this point, your career goals and aspirations should be jelling. At the very least, you should have a plan for finding out more information. And don't forget about networking, which was covered in more detail in chapter 2. Remember to research the school or degree program before you reach out and especially before you visit. Faculty and staff find students who ask challenging questions much more impressive than those who ask questions that can be answered by spending ten minutes on the school website.

Chapter 4 goes into detail about the next steps—writing a résumé and cover letter, interviewing well, follow-up communications, and more. This information is not just for college grads; you can use it to secure internships, volunteer positions, summer jobs, and more. In fact, the sooner you can hone these communication skills, the better off you'll be in the professional world, regardless of your job.

4

Writing Your Résumé and Interviewing

No matter what you aspire to be, having a well-written résumé and impeccable interviewing skills will help you reach your ultimate goals. This chapter provides some helpful tips and advice to build the best résumé and cover letter, how to interview well with all your prospective employers, and how to communicate effectively and professionally at all times. The advice in this chapter isn't just for people entering the workforce full-time, either; it can help you score that internship or summer job or help you give a great college interview to impress the admissions office.

This chapter also discusses important interviewing skills that you can build and develop over time and includes some tips for dealing successfully with stress, which is an inevitable by-product of a busy life.

Which job will be right for you? ©*metamorworks/iStock/Getty Images Plus*

Finding and Applying for the Job

To apply for a job, you first have to know where to look for one. One of the quickest ways to find out what jobs are available in your field is to simply Google it (or search the internet with whichever search engine you like best).

Online Job Sites

When companies want to hire new employees, they post job descriptions on job-hunting or employee recruitment websites. These are a fantastic resource long before you're ready to actually apply for a job. You can read real job descriptions for real jobs and see what qualifications and experience are needed for the kinds of jobs you're interested in. You'll also get a good idea of the range of salaries and benefits that go with different types of marketing professions.

Pay attention to the required qualifications, of course, but also pay attention to the desired qualifications—these are the ones you don't *have* to have, but if you have them, you'll have an edge over other applicants.

Here are a few sites to get you started:

- www.monster.com
- www.indeed.com
- www.ziprecruiter.com
- www.glassdoor.com
- www.simplyhired.com

Professional Organizations

One of the services provided by most professional organizations is a list of open positions. Employers post jobs here because organization members are often the most qualified and experienced. The Resources section in this book lists professional organizations for the different marketing professions discussed in the book. For other professions, check online and talk to people in your field (such as your professors) to find out which organizations to join and where the best source of job information is likely to be.

Networking

Some say the best way to find a job is through networking. Your personal and professional contacts may know about an upcoming job that hasn't even been advertised yet. Sometimes an employer may even create a position for someone they want to hire. Keep in touch with the people you know in the field, at every level, and let them know that you're available.

> **Tip:** If you know someone who already works at the company/organization, ask her for some inside advice and find out whether it's okay to mention her name during the interview. If the interviewer finds out you know someone who works there, that can really work in your favor.

Still wondering about how to network? Flip back to the end of chapter 2 and read the section devoted to networking for some useful tips.

MELISA DUFFY: MARKETING DIRECTOR IN PUBLISHING

Melisa Duffy earned her bachelor's degree in business administration and economics from Indiana State University. She is currently a marketing director for a publishing company. She manages a team of product marketers, publicity managers, and channel marketing managers and dips into most of those roles daily as well. The product marketers are responsible for positioning products and creating awareness with consumers. The publicity managers work with media, bloggers, and industry organizations to generate and place stories for products. The channel marketing managers work directly with accounts such as Amazon and Target to maximize promotional opportunities and convert shoppers into purchasers. The best part of managing a team is guiding colleagues in development and watching successful campaign creation.

After working in a variety of roles in marketing—including assistant, coordinator, brand manager, product marketing manager, communications manager, and channel marketing manager—over the past thirty years, she enjoys the fact that she can be a hands-on manager and help colleagues, as she has been in most of these roles at some point in her career.

Can you explain how you ended up in this field? What about it interested you? Is it what you expected it would be?

I have always enjoyed retail and merchandising. My first "real" job was working at a retail store—the absolute best way to find out what I enjoyed (helping match a customer need to the product) and what I did not enjoy (managing customer complaints). When I entered college and decided to major in business, the degree required introductory courses in all the functional areas of business accounting, finance, management, marketing, and informatics (the early form of computer science). I found the marketing courses the most enjoyable. I enjoyed discovering how to message a product to customers in a way that caught their attention and made them stop and ask for more information. The tool set for a marketer has changed tremendously over the years, but the core skill for any marketer is understanding who the customer is for your product or service and finding a way to communicate that message somehow that entices the customer to ask for more information or make a purchase.

What's a "typical" day in your job? What do you do day to day?

I like to say a typical day is part strategy and part tactical and is likely a good mix for any marketer. Typically, we spend part of the day working on long-term projects, such as campaigns—campaigns always involve strategy, goals, and results, so spending part of the day analyzing where the team is with larger campaigns is a big part of the day. From a tactical standpoint, marketing teams tend to shoulder a lot of work. It is not uncommon to write promotional copy for ads, help answer a customer's question, work with various sales teams to position products and provide additional information to close a sale, analyze results from a current campaign, and attend a lot of meetings. Marketing tends to get invited to a lot of meetings and that is a common theme in every industry.

What is the best part of being in this field?

The best part of being in marketing is being able to use the creative side of your brain as well as the analytical side. Marketing gets to dip into each area and find the best mix for communicating and positioning products and then deciding the measurement of success. Marketing is usually the closest team that works with customers, and the insights customers share make products better. If you enjoy listening as much as you enjoy talking, marketing offers the best of both.

What's the greatest challenge the market faces at this time? What are your greatest challenges day in and day out?

The biggest challenges for marketers is the ever-evolving tools and tool sets we are expected to use. To launch a campaign, it is not uncommon to work with five to six tools, and those five to six tools change every few years. Dedicating a portion of the role to continuous learning and training is necessary but challenging, as the role of marketing is one that is very busy in any organization. Within a few years, the tools you learned in college, with rare exception, are not ones that you will use in your day-to-day. Another big challenge is that marketing has become a job of specialists rather than generalists. When I started my career, the marketing manager did every aspect of the role, but as marketing became driven by technology, specialists emerged within SEO, copy, content, analytics, and so on. Creating and launching a marketing plan or campaign takes a lot of collaboration and communication with so many specialties.

What has been most surprising about your career path?

The most surprising part of my career path is that I have stayed in the same industry for most of my career but held many different marketing roles that were functionally very different.

Do you think your education adequately prepared you for your current job?

I was lucky in that education allowed me to find the area of business I enjoyed, and I was able to find a job in the field of marketing. What is most interesting is that within five years, no one asks about education—all an employer wants to see is experience. Education opens the door to the role, but after that you need to continue to gain skills that companies want.

Where do you see this field going in the future?

Marketing has become very data and metric driven. The tools to gather data and make decisions have become part of a marketer's work flow each day. The field will continue to evolve to data-driven marketing and continuous analysis of the results of your marketing—from clicks to conversions, you must communicate results more often.

What traits or skills make for a good marketing professional?

The ability to listen to others and absorb information is critical. Good marketers pick up nuances in customer conversations and behaviors and turn those into competitive advantages. Communication is important in all areas of business, but especially in marketing. Communication—both written and verbal—is critical, and you must be able to do both well.

What advice do you have for young people considering this career?

Decide what you like to do and what you are good at doing. Marketing has become a role of specialists and it is likely you will have a well-defined role within a marketing department. It is always easy to spot what marketers enjoy most about their roles. I work with marketers who love data and will spend hours in programs finding patterns. I also have marketers who love to write and communicate, and they are the first to create and present to other teams. Also, do some research on job sites and really look at how companies position the roles within marketing and what the requirements are for those roles. Be ready to continually update your skills. To stay ahead in marketing, you should expect to be spending a portion of your time learning new tools and ways to market.

Writing Your Résumé

If you're a teen writing a résumé for your first job, you likely don't have a lot of work experience under your belt yet. Because of this limited work experience, you need to include classes and coursework that are related to the job you're seeking, any school activities and volunteer experience you have, and your best sample work. While you are writing your résumé, you might discover some talents and recall some activities you did that you forgot about but that are still important to add. Think about volunteer work, side jobs you've held, organizations you've been a member of, and the like.

Parts of a Résumé

The functional résumé is the best approach when you don't have a lot of pertinent work experience, as it is written to highlight your abilities rather than your experience. (The other, perhaps more common, type of résumé is called the chronological résumé, which lists a person's accomplishments in chronological order, most recent jobs listed first.) This section breaks down and discusses the functional résumé in greater detail.

NAME SURNAME

PROFESSION

CONTACTS

- +123.456.7890
- 123456, Address, City, State
- youremail@mail.com
- www.yourweb.com

SKILLS

Skill #1
Skill #2
Skill #3
Skill #4
Skill #5

SOFTWARE

Software #1
Software #2
Software #3
Software #4

LANGUAGES

English
French
Chinese

INTERESTS

Lorem ipsum dolor sit amet, consectetur adipiscing elit. Pellentesque ac dolor sit amet quam fermentum tempus.

Lorem ipsum dolor sit amet, consectetur adipiscing elit. Pellentesque ac dolor sit amet quam fermentum tempus.

Lorem ipsum dolor sit amet, consectetur adipiscing elit. Pellentesque ac dolor sit amet quam fermentum tempus.

PROFESSIONAL PROFILE

Lorem ipsum dolor sit amet, consectetur adipiscing elit. Pellentesque ac dolor sit amet quam fermentum tempus. Fusce ullamcorper gravida consequat. Phasellus mollis interdum lacus, vitae fermentum est luctus quis. In sed quam ac neque ornare egestas. Maecenas efficitur imperdiet sem in maximus. Fusce vitae augue ullamcorper, elementum velit sed, aliquam metus. Donec ut mollis orci. Etiam enim eros, tristique interdum malesuada non, tincidunt et sapien. Nunc sodales ante nec mi volutpat varius. Ut ac eros vel arcu efficitur blandit vel et leo. Cras in rhoncus dolor. Praesent pulvinar velit sed diam laoreet condimentum. Vestibulum scelerisque lorem non nibh faucibus condimentum. Suspendisse vel magna malesuada, scelerisque sapien sit amet, sodales orci.

Quisque convallis auctor libero eget vehicula. Suspendisse nisi turpis, convallis nec nulla ac, bibendum sodales tortor. Duis et velit nunc. Nulla ullamcorper augue eu odio accumsan posuere vel sed metus. Nam ac velit lacinia, molestie justo a, luctus purus. Aenean pellentesque nunc at elit volutpat aliquet. Suspendisse potenti. Pellentesque habitant morbi tristique senectus et netus et malesuada fames ac turpis egestas. Phasellus quis vehicula dolor, non aliquet ipsum. Ut mauris mauris, finibus non mattis vitae, pulvinar ornare ante. Sed nec porta elit.

EDUCATION

2001-2005 DEGREE / MAJOR
University / School Name
Lorem ipsum dolor sit amet, consectetur adipiscing elit. Pellentesque ac dolor sit amet quam fermentum tempus. Fusce ullamcorper gravida consequat. Phasellus mollis interdum lacus, vitae fermentum est luctus quis. In sed quam ac neque ornare egestas.

2006-2010 DEGREE / MAJOR
University / School Name
Lorem ipsum dolor sit amet, consectetur adipiscing elit. Pellentesque ac dolor sit amet quam fermentum tempus. Fusce ullamcorper gravida consequat. Phasellus mollis interdum lacus, vitae fermentum est luctus quis. In sed quam ac neque ornare egestas.

WORK EXPERIENCE

2018 -Present COMPANY NAME / POSITION
Lorem ipsum dolor sit amet, consectetur adipiscing elit. Pellentesque ac dolor sit amet quam fermentum tempus. Fusce ullamcorper gravida consequat. Phasellus mollis interdum lacus, vitae fermentum est luctus quis. In sed quam ac neque ornare egestas. Maecenas efficitur imperdiet sem in maximus. Fusce vitae augue ullamcorper, elementum velit sed, aliquam metus.

2018 -2015 COMPANY NAME / POSITION
Lorem ipsum dolor sit amet, consectetur adipiscing elit. Pellentesque ac dolor sit amet quam fermentum tempus. Fusce ullamcorper gravida consequat. Phasellus mollis interdum lacus, vitae fermentum est luctus quis. In sed quam ac neque ornare egestas. Maecenas efficitur imperdiet sem in maximus. Fusce vitae augue ullamcorper, elementum velit sed, aliquam metus.

2018 -2015 COMPANY NAME / POSITION
Lorem ipsum dolor sit amet, consectetur adipiscing elit. Pellentesque ac dolor sit amet quam fermentum tempus. Fusce ullamcorper gravida consequat. Phasellus mollis interdum lacus, vitae fermentum est luctus quis. In sed quam ac neque ornare egestas. Maecenas efficitur imperdiet sem in maximus. Fusce vitae augue ullamcorper, elementum velit sed, aliquam metus.

ACHIEVEMENTS

2015 ACHIEVEMENT #1
Lorem ipsum dolor sit amet, consectetur adipiscing elit. Pellentesque ac dolor sit amet quam fermentum tempus.

2017 ACHIEVEMENT #2
Lorem ipsum dolor sit amet, consectetur adipiscing elit. Pellentesque ac dolor sit amet quam fermentum tempus.

REFERENCES

Reference Name
Position title
referencename@mail.com
+123.456.7890

Reference Name
Position title
referencename@mail.com
+123.456.7890

Reference Name
Position title
referencename@mail.com
+123.456.7890

As someone in a creative field, you should have a résumé that is visually compelling and unique.
©Vera Fedorova/iStock/Getty Images Plus

Here are some typical parts of a résumé:

- *Heading:* This should include your name, address, and contact information, including phone, e-mail, and portfolio website if you have one.
- *Education:* Always list your most recent school or program first. Include date of completion (or expected date of graduation), degree or certificate earned, and the institution's name and address. Include workshops, seminars, and related classes here as well.
- *Skills:* Skills include computer literacy, leadership skills, organizational skills, and time-management skills. Be specific in this area, when possible.
- *Activities:* Activities can be related to skills. Perhaps an activity listed here helped you develop a skill listed above. This section can be combined with the Skills section, but it's often helpful to break these apart if you have enough substantive things to say in both areas. Examples include leadership roles, community service work, clubs and organizations, and so on.
- *Experience:* If you don't have any actual work experience that's relevant, you might consider skipping this section. However, you can list any marketing or advertising work you've done if you have relevant work to show.
- *Interests:* This section is optional, but it's a chance to include special talents and interests. Keep it short, factual, and specific.
- *Languages:* List any scripting and programming languages you've used, as well as relevant software such as Photoshop, Acrobat, InDesign, and so on.
- *References:* It's best to say that references are available on request. If you do list actual contacts, list no more than three and make sure you inform them that they might be contacted.

The Skills, Interests, Experience, and Languages sections can be creatively combined or developed to maximize your abilities and experience. These are not set-in-stone sections that every résumé must have.

If you're still not seeing the big picture here, it's helpful to look at résumé and portfolio examples online to see how others have approached this process.

Search for "marketing résumé examples" or "example portfolios" to get a look at some examples.

Résumé-Writing Tips

Regardless of your situation and the reason you're writing the résumé, here are some basic tips and techniques you should use:

- Keep it short, attractive, and compelling. Your design can be unique and clever, but make sure it doesn't get in the way of readability.
- Use simple language. Keep it to one page.
- Highlight your academic achievements, such as a high GPA (above 3.5) or academic awards. If you have taken classes related to the job you're interviewing for, list those briefly as well.
- Emphasize your extracurricular activities, internships, and the like. Use these activities to show your skills, interests, and abilities.
- Use action verbs, such as *led, designed, created, taught, ran,* and *developed.*
- Be specific and give examples.
- Always be honest.
- Include leadership roles and experience.
- Edit and proofread at least twice and have someone else do the same. Ask a professional (such as your school writing center or your local library services) to proofread it for you also. Don't forget to run spell check.
- In some cases, include a cover letter (discussed next).

The Cover Letter

Every résumé you send out via standard mail should include a cover letter. This can be the most important part of your job search because it's often the first thing that potential employers read. By including the cover letter, you're showing potential employers that you took the time to learn about them and address them personally. This goes a long way to show that you're interested in the position.

Be sure to call the organization or verify on the website the name and title of the person to whom you should address the letter. This letter should be brief. Introduce yourself and begin with a statement that will grab the person's attention. Keep in mind that employers will potentially receive hundreds of résumés and cover letters for every open position. You want yours to stand out. Important information to include in the cover letter, from the top, includes:

- The current date
- Your address and contact information
- The recipient's name, company name, and contact information
- Salutation

Then you begin the letter portion of the cover letter, which should mention how you heard about the position, something extra about you that will interest the potential employer, practical skills you can bring to the position, and past experience related to the job. You should apply the facts outlined in your résumé to the job to which you're applying. Each cover letter should be personalized for the position and company to which you're applying. Don't use "To whom it may concern"; instead, take the time to find out to whom you should actually address the letter. Finally, end with a closing, such as "Sincerely, Piper E. Smith," and be sure to add your signature. Search the internet for "sample cover letters for internships" or "sample cover letters for high schoolers" to see some good examples.

When you are e-mailing your résumé, you'll need to pay particular attention to the subject line of your e-mail. Be sure that it is specific to the position you are applying for. In fact, you should follow all the guidelines discussed in the above paragraphs for creating a cover letter when you write your introductory e-mail.

In all cases, it's really important to follow the employer's instructions on how to submit your cover letter and résumé. Generally speaking, it is better to send PDF documents rather than editable documents. For one, everyone can read a PDF, whereas they might not be able to read the version of Word that you used. Most word processing programs have an option under the Save command that allows you to save your work as a PDF.

LINKING IN WITH IMPACT

As well as your paper or electronic résumé, creating a LinkedIn profile is a good way to highlight your experience and promote yourself as well as to network. Joining professional organizations and connecting with other people in your desired field are good ways to keep abreast of changes and trends and work opportunities.

The key elements of a LinkedIn profile are your photo, your headline, and your profile summary. These are the most revealing parts of the profile and the ones on which employers and connections will base their impression of you.

The photo should be carefully chosen. Remember that LinkedIn is not Facebook or Instagram: It is not the place to share a photo of you acting too casually on vacation or at a party. According to Joshua Waldman, author of *Job Searching with Social Media for Dummies*, the choice of photo should be taken seriously and be done right. His tips:

- Choose a photo in which you have a nice smile.
- Dress in professional clothing.
- Be sure the background of the photo is pleasing to the eye. According to Waldman, some colors—like green and blue—convey a feeling of trust and stability.
- Remember: it's not a mug shot. You can be creative with the angle of your photo rather than staring directly into the camera.
- Use your photo to convey some aspect of your personality.
- Focus on your face. Remember: visitors to your profile will see only a small thumbnail image, so be sure your face takes up most of it.[1]

Interviewing Skills

The best way to avoid nerves and keep calm when you're interviewing is to be prepared. It's okay to feel scared, but keep it in perspective. It's likely that you'll receive many more rejections than acceptances in your professional life, as we all do. However, you only need one *yes* to start out.

Think of the interviewing process as a learning experience. With the right attitude, you will learn from each one and get better with each subsequent interview. That should be your overarching goal. Consider these tips and tricks when interviewing, whether it be for a job, internship, college admission, or something else entirely:

- Practice interviewing with a friend or relative. Practicing will help calm your nerves and make you feel more prepared. Ask for specific feedback from your friends. Do you need to speak more loudly? Are you making enough eye contact? Are you actively listening when the other person is speaking?
- Learn as much as you can about the company or organization. Also be sure to understand the position for which you're applying. This will show the interviewer that you are motivated and interested in their organization.
- Speak up during the interview. Convey to the interviewer important points about you. Don't be afraid to ask questions. Try to remember the interviewers' names and call them by name. Consider these questions:
  - What created the need to fill this position? Is it a new position or has someone left the company?
  - Where does this position fit in the overall hierarchy of the organization?
  - What are the key skills required to succeed in this job?
  - What challenges might I expect to face within the first six months on the job?
  - How does this position relate to the achievement of the company's (or department's or boss's) goals?
  - How would you describe the company culture?
- Arrive early dressed professionally and appropriately (you can read more about proper dress in later in the chapter).
- Take some time to prepare answers to commonly asked questions. Be ready to describe your career or educational goals to the interviewer.[2]

Common questions you may be asked during a job interview include:

- Tell me about yourself.
- What are your greatest strengths?

- What are your weaknesses?
- Tell me something about yourself that's not on your résumé.
- What are your career goals?
- How do you handle failure? Are you willing to fail?
- How do you handle stress and pressure?
- What are you passionate about?
- Why do you want to work for us?

Common questions you may be asked during a college admissions interview include:

- Tell me about yourself.
- Why are you interested in going to college?
- Why do you want to major in this subject?
- What are your academic strengths?
- What are your academic weaknesses? How have you addressed them?
- What will you contribute to this college/school/university?
- Where do you see yourself in ten years?
- How do you handle failure? Are you willing to fail?
- How do you handle stress and pressure?
- Whom do you most admire?
- What is your favorite book?
- What do you do for fun?
- Why are you interested in this college/school/university?

Jot down notes about your answers to these questions, but don't try to memorize the answers. You don't want to come off as too rehearsed during the interview. Remember to be as specific and detailed as possible when answering these questions. Your goal is to set yourself apart in some way from the other interviewees. Always accentuate the positive, even when you're asked about something you did not like, or about failure or stress. Most importantly, though, be yourself.

Tip: Active listening is the process of fully concentrating on what is being said, understanding it, and providing nonverbal cues and responses to the person talking.[3] It's the opposite of being distracted and thinking about something else when someone is talking. Active listening takes practice. You might find that your mind wanders and you need to bring it back to the person talking (and this could happen multiple times during one conversation). Practice this technique in regular conversations with friends and relatives. In addition to helping you give a better interview, it can cut down on nerves and make you more popular with friends and family, as everyone wants to feel that they are really being heard. For more on active listening, check out www .mindtools.com/CommSkll/ActiveListening.htm.

You should also be ready to ask questions of your interviewer. In a practical sense, there should be some questions you have that you can't find the answer to on the website or in the literature. Also, asking questions shows that you are interested and have done your homework. Avoid asking questions about salary/scholarships or special benefits at this stage, and don't ask about anything negative that you've heard about the company. Keep the questions positive and related to yourself and the position to which you're applying. Some examples of questions to ask potential employers include:

- What is a typical career path for a person in this position?
- How would you describe the ideal candidate for this position?
- How is the department organized?
- What kind of responsibilities come with this job? (Don't ask this if it has already been addressed in the job description or discussion.)
- What can I do as a follow-up?
- When do you expect to reach a decision?

This advice on interviewing is pertinent to college visits too! See the section "Make the Most of School Visits" in chapter 3 for some good example questions to ask the college admissions office. The important thing is to write your own questions related to information you really want to know, and be sure your question isn't already answered on the website, in the job description, or in the literature. This will show genuine interest.

TO SHAKE OR NOT TO SHAKE?

Shaking hands in the twenty-first century is something to think about. ©*PeopleImages /iStock/Getty Images Plus*

A handshake is a traditional form of greeting, especially in business. When you arrive for a job interview—or just meet someone new—a good firm handshake shows that you are a person to be taken seriously.

But shaking hands is not done in every culture, and even in North America, the norm of shaking hands has changed. During the COVID-19 crisis, people stopped shaking hands in order to avoid spreading germs. As things get back to normal, some people will want to résumé shaking hands and some people won't.

When you arrive for a job interview, follow the lead of the person you're meeting with. A respectful head nod is just fine.

Dressing Appropriately

It's important to determine what kind of dress is appropriate in the setting of the interview. What is appropriate in a large corporate setting might be different from what you'd expect at a small liberal arts college or at a creative design firm. For example, most college admissions offices suggest business casual attire, for example, but depending on the job interview, you may want to step it up from there. Again, it's important to do your homework and be prepared. In addition to reading up on the organization's guidelines, it never hurts to take a look around the website to see what other people are wearing to work or to interviews. *If you're not sure, remember that it's better to be overdressed than underdressed.*

In general, business casual means less formal than business attire, like a suit, but a step up from jeans, a T-shirt, and sneakers.

- *For men:* You can't go wrong with khaki pants, a polo or button-up shirt, and brown or black shoes.
- *For women:* Nice slacks, a shirt or blouse that isn't too revealing, and nice flats or shoes with a heel that's not too high.

> **Tip:** You may want to find out in advance whether the organization has a dress code. Don't hesitate to ask the person who's going to interview you if you're unsure what to wear. You can also call the main number and ask the receptionist what people typically wear to interviews.

Regardless of the setting, make sure your clothes are not wrinkled, untidy, or stained. Avoid revealing clothing of any kind.

Follow-Up Communication

Be sure to follow up, whether via e-mail or regular mail, with a thank-you note to the interviewer. This is true whether you're interviewing for a job or interviewing with a college. A handwritten thank-you note, posted in the mail, is best. In addition to showing consideration, it will trigger the interviewer's memory about you and it shows that you have genuine interest in the position, company, or school. Be sure to follow the business letter format and highlight the key points of your interview and experience at the company or university.

Even something like "business casual" can be interpreted in many ways, so do some research to find out what exactly is expected of you. ©*seb_ra/iStock/Getty Images Plus*

Be prompt with your thank-you note! Put it in the mail the day after your interview or send it by e-mail the same day.

EFFECTIVELY HANDLING STRESS

As you're forging ahead with your life plans—whether it's college, a full-time job, or even a gap year—you might find that these decisions feel very important and heavy and that the stress is difficult to deal with. This is completely normal. Try these simple techniques to relieve stress:

- Take deep breaths in and out. Try this for thirty seconds. You'll be amazed at how it can help.
- Close your eyes and clear your mind.
- Go scream at a passing subway car. Or lock yourself in a closet and scream. Or scream into a pillow. For some people, this can really help.
- Keep the issue in perspective. Any decision you make now can be changed if it doesn't work out.

Want to know how to avoid stress altogether? It is surprisingly simple. Of course, simple doesn't always mean easy, but these ideas are basic and make sense based on what we know about the human body:

- Get enough sleep.
- Eat healthy.
- Get exercise.
- Go outside.
- Schedule downtime.
- Set healthy boundaries with work and other obligations.
- Connect with friends and family.

The bottom line is that you need to take time for self-care. There will always be stress in life, but how you deal with it makes all the difference. This only becomes more important as you enter college or the workforce and maybe have a family. Developing good, consistent habits related to self-care now will serve you all your life.

What Employers Expect

Regardless of the job, profession, or field, there are universal characteristics that all employers—and schools, for that matter—look for in candidates. At this early stage in your professional life, you have an opportunity to recognize which of these foundational characteristics are your strengths (and therefore highlight them in an interview) and which are weaknesses (and therefore continue to work on them and build them up). Consider these characteristics:

- Positive attitude
- Dependability
- Desire to continue to learn
- Initiative
- Effective communication
- Cooperation

- Organization
- Passion for the profession

This is not an exhaustive list, and other characteristics can very well include things like creativity, sensitivity to others, honesty, good judgment, loyalty, responsibility, and punctuality. Consider these important characteristics when you answer the common questions that employers ask. It pays to work these traits into the answers—of course, being honest and realistic about yourself.

BEWARE WHAT YOU SHARE ON SOCIAL MEDIA

Most of us engage in social media. Sites such as Facebook, Twitter, and Instagram provide a platform for sharing photos and memories, opinions and life events, and reveal everything from our political stance to our sense of humor. It's a great way to connect with people around the world, but once you post something, it's accessible to anyone—including potential employers—unless you take mindful precautions.

Your posts may be public, which means you may be making the wrong impression without realizing it. More and more often, people are using search engines like Google to get a sense of potential employers, colleagues, or employees, and the impression you make online can have a strong impact on how you are perceived. According to the website CareerBuilder, 60 percent of employers search for information on candidates on social media sites.[4]

The website Glassdoor offers the following tips for how to keep your social media activity from sabotaging your career success:

1. Check your privacy settings. Ensure that your photos and posts are accessible only to the friends or contacts you want to see them. You want to come across as professional and reliable.
2. Rather than avoiding social media while searching for a job, use it to your advantage. Give future employees a sense of your professional interest by liking pages or joining groups of professional organizations related to your career goals.
3. Grammar counts. Be attentive to the quality of writing of all your posts and comments.

4. Be consistent. With each social media outlet, there is a different focus and tone of what you are communicating. LinkedIn is very professional while Facebook is far more social and relaxed. It's okay to take a different tone on various social media sites, but be sure you aren't blatantly contradicting yourself.
5. Choose your username carefully. Remember, social media may be the first impression anyone has of you in the professional realm.[5]

JENNIFER RYDER: MARKETING MANAGER AT A SMALL COMPANY

Jennifer Ryder. *Courtesy of Jennifer Ryder*

Jennifer Ryder earned her bachelor's degree in psychology from Cleveland State University. She currently works as a marketing manager for WXZ Development, Inc., overseeing all aspects of marketing for the company. Additionally, her responsibilities include managing the property management department and assisting the owner with day-to-day planning.

Although it may seem like she made a wrong turn, Jennifer believes it is her degree in psychology that has allowed her to be able to continually pivot when life throws her curveballs. Having a background in human behavior certainly helps when communicating with her team and understanding how to have everyone's needs met. She enjoys the freedom that working for a small company offers, like spending time with her family, dogs, and vacations. Did she mention they do not have to wear suits to work either? That is a real plus!

Can you explain how you ended up in this field? What about it interested you? Is it what you expected it would be?

My path to marketing has been a zigzag approach, as marketing was not my first choice nor the degree I pursued in college. I have a bachelor's degree in psychology and was a social worker for the first eight years after college. After that, I became a fundraiser for nonprofits, where I raised money and later worked with corporations that gave money to charities. After leaving corporate America, I found a small family-owned business where I discovered that I could use all of my skills and creativity to help further their overall brand as well as launch new initiatives.

What's a "typical" day in your job? What do you do day to day?

The beauty of my job is that there is no "typical" day. This is something that I really enjoy about the job. My week can consist of website design/updates, social media ads/postings, website analytics, print media efforts, working with interior designers, photographers, etc. It is always changing and evolving, which keeps things very interesting.

What is the best part of being in this field?

It is always evolving. There are some standards that remain, but it is certainly not something that holds back ideas or creativity.

What's the greatest challenge the market faces at this time? What are your greatest challenges day in and day out?

This past year, COVID was our biggest challenge, because it forced more need for online presence and analytics/SEO (search engine optimization) work.

My biggest challenge is the social media aspect. I prefer handing that over to someone younger who is more in tune with it.

What has been most surprising about your career path?

That I am actually really good at it even though it wasn't something I ever even considered doing.

Where do you see this field going in the future?

I think marketing can be anything in the future, especially as technology progresses and we are able to reach more people across the globe.

What traits or skills make for a good marketing professional?

You need to be a planner and be organized. Being a good listener is also important, as well as being creative.

What advice do you have for young people considering this career?

Think about how you want to spend your day at your future job. Is that at a desk, or traveling, or dressing up for work every day? Do you want a high-stress or low-stress position? Do you see yourself giving lots of presentations? I never considered those are things when I thought about a career. If I had thought about what I wanted in other respects, like a family some day or to dress casually, it may have made me rethink my career path.

How can a young person prepare for a career in marketing while in high school?
There are so many aspects to marketing, such as digital/print/social/advertising, and so on. I would recommend shadowing a professional for a week or trying to get a job/summer internship doing social media posts at a local business. Then you will know better if it is something you would want to pursue in college.

Tip: *Personal contacts can make the difference!* Don't be afraid to contact marketing professionals you know. Personal connections can be a great way to find jobs and internship opportunities. Your high school teachers, your coaches and mentors, and your friends' parents are all examples of people who very well may know about jobs or opportunities that would suit you. Start asking several months before you hope to start a job or internship, because it will take some time to do research and arrange interviews. You can also use social media in your search. LinkedIn (www.linkedin .com), for example, includes lots of searchable information on local companies. Follow and interact with people on social media to get their attention. Just remember to act professionally and communicate with proper grammar, just as you would in person.

Summary

Well, you made it to the end of this book! Hopefully, you have learned enough about the fields in marketing to start your journey or to continue along your path. If you've reached the end and you feel like some form of marketing is your passion, that's great news. If you've figured out that it isn't the right field for you, that's good information to learn too. For many of us, figuring out what we *don't* want to do and what we *don't* like are important steps in finding the right career.

A career in marketing awaits! ©*Harbucks/iStock/Getty Images Plus*

There is a lot of good news about the field of marketing. It's a great career choice for anyone with a passion for communication. It's also a great career for people who get energy from working in creative settings. Job demand is good and growing. Having a plan and an idea about your future can help guide your decisions. After reading this book, you should be well on your way to having a plan for your future. Good luck to you as you move ahead!

Glossary

2D animation: A type of animation in which the images are "flat," meaning they have width and height but no depth.

3D animation: A type of animation in which images appear in a three-dimensional space, with width, height, and depth.

accreditation: The act of officially recognizing an organizational body, person, or educational facility as having a particular status or being qualified to perform a particular activity. For example, schools and colleges are accredited. *See also* **certification**.

Acrobat: An Adobe document-management program that enables users to create, edit, and manage documents in Portable Document Format (PDF). PDF documents look the same regardless of which operating system or hardware setup is used to view it.

ACT: One of the standardized college entrance tests that anyone wanting to enter undergraduate studies in the United States should take. It measures knowledge and skills in mathematics, English, reading, and science reasoning as they apply to college readiness. The ACT includes four multiple-choice sections and an optional writing test. The total score of the ACT is 36. *See also* **SAT**.

Adobe suite of products: The industry standard applications for many graphic design jobs; includes Photoshop, Illustrator, Dreamweaver, Acrobat, and InDesign.

associate degree: A degree awarded by a community or junior college that typically requires two years of study; however, this can vary by the degree earned and the university awarding the degree.

bachelor's degree: An undergraduate degree awarded by a college or university that typically requires a four-year course of study when pursued full-time, but can vary by the degree earned and the university awarding the degree.

body of work: All of the pieces ever made by a single artist (sometimes called the artist's *oeuvre*).

brand marketing: A type of marketing that promotes products or services in a way that highlights the overall brand. A company's *brand* represents their identity: who they are, what they do, what kind of quality they provide, their reputation for trustworthiness, and more.

business model: A map for the successful creation and operation of a business, including sources of revenue, target customer base, products, and details of financing.

certification: The action or process of confirming that an individual has acquired certain skills or knowledge, usually provided by some third-party review, assessment, or educational body. Individuals, not organizations, are certified. *See also* **accreditation**.

content creation specialists: Workers who create content strategies, research trending topics, and write content for online use. Those who thrive in this profession have great writing skills and a strong ability to market their work.

cover letter: A document that usually accompanies a résumé and allows candidates applying to a job or a school or internship an opportunity to describe their motivation and qualifications.

creative: Having the ability to make something that did not previously exist; also used in the business world to refer to a person who does creative work, such as a graphic artist or web designer.

criticism: The discussion or evaluation of a creative work, usually in terms of its perceived quality.

critique: The process of describing and analyzing a creative work. In the classroom, critiques are a regular part of the learning process in which the teacher and other students give their responses to a particular piece and discuss its qualities, both positive and negative. It is a useful process for both those giving and those receiving the critique.

deadlines: Targets set relating to when particular tasks need to be completed.

digital images: A computer file consisting of picture elements called pixels. "High resolution" digital images usually have at least 300 pixels per square inch at full size and are used for printed images. "Low resolution" digital images usually have 72 pixels per square inch and are used online. Common digital image types are JPG, PNG, TIFF, GIF, and PostScript.

digital marketing professionals: Workers who develop effective marketing campaigns online and translate business goals into successful marketing campaigns. Their goals usually include increasing brand awareness, promoting company products or services, and driving up sales.

doctoral degree: The highest level of degree awarded by colleges and universities. This degree qualifies the holder to teach at the university level and requires (usually published) research in the field. Earning a doctoral degree typically requires an additional three to five years of study after earning a bachelor's degree. Anyone with a doctoral degree—not just medical doctors—can be addressed as a "doctor."

e-mail marketing: The process of sending a commercial message, typically to a group of people, using e-mail. In the most general sense, every e-mail sent to a potential or current customer can be considered e-mail marketing. It involves the use of e-mail to send advertisements, request business, inform subscribers about news, or solicit sales or donations.

entrepreneur: A person who starts, organizes, and manages a business (often a new business) and is responsible for the financial risk involved.

freelancer: A person who works independently in a business providing services for a variety of clients.

gap year: A year between high school and college (or sometimes between college and postgraduate studies) during which the student is not in school but is instead involved in other pursuits, typically volunteer programs such as the Peace Corps, travel, or work and teaching.

general educational development (GED): A certificate earned by someone who has not graduated from high school that is the equivalent to a high school diploma.

Google Analytics: A web analytics service offered by Google that tracks and reports website traffic. Web analytics professionals use this tool to collect data about website visitors, such as how many people come to the site, how long they stay, which pages they visit, which areas they click, and so on. This data may be analyzed to improve a website, sell more product, or determine ROI on advertising and other marketing efforts. Other options include Adobe Web Analytics, Watson Customer Experience Analytics by IBM, Mixpanel, and Webtrends Analytics.

grants: Money to pay for postsecondary education that is typically awarded to students who have financial need, but can also be used in the areas of athletics, academics, demographics, veteran support, and special talents. Grants do not have to be paid back.

Hypertext Markup Language (HTML): A simple markup language used to control how web pages look in a browser. It can be enhanced by using cascading style sheets and scripting languages such as JavaScript.

master's degree: A postgraduate degree awarded by colleges and universities that requires at least one additional year of study after obtaining a bachelor's degree. The degree holder shows mastery of a specific field.

multimedia art: Artwork created with new media technologies and computers.

online portfolio: An organized presentation of creative work on a website, blog, or social media site.

paid search/pay-per-click (PPC): An internet advertising model used to encourage traffic to websites, in which the advertiser pays the publisher of the web page when the ad is clicked. Pay-per-click is commonly associated with first-tier search engines. Search returns with the word "ad" at the top are examples of PPCs.

personal statement: A written description of your accomplishments, outlook, interests, goals, and personality that is an important part of your college application. The personal statement should set you apart from other applicants. The required length depends on the institution, but they generally range from one to two pages, or 500–1,000 words.

Photoshop: An Adobe illustration and design tool that enables users to create and edit computer graphics images that are in the raster graphics format (essentially, JPEG, PING, or GIF). Most of its features are built for editing and retouching digital photographs; however, Photoshop can also edit digital video frames, render text, create 3D modeling features, and develop design elements content for websites. Like most of Adobe's products, it is geared toward use by professionals.

portfolio: A collection of work selected by a creative person to share with potential clients or associates that best represents the creator's style and current work.

postsecondary degree: An educational degree above and beyond a high school education. This is a general description that includes trade certificates and certifications; associate, bachelor's, and master's degrees; and beyond.

SAT: One of the standardized tests in the United States that anyone applying to undergraduate studies should take. It measures verbal and mathematical reasoning abilities as they relate to predicting successful performance in college. It is intended to complement a student's GPA and school record in assessing readiness for college. The total score of the SAT is 1600. *See also* **ACT**.

scholarships: Merit-based aid used to pay for postsecondary education that does not have to be paid back. Scholarships are typically awarded based on academic excellence or some other special talent, such as music or art.

search engine optimization (SEO): The practice of improving the visitor traffic (the quality and quantity of visitors) to a website or web page from search engines.[1] SEO is specifically through nonpaid (also known as "organic") search engine results. *See also* **web analytics specialists** and **paid search/pay-per-click (PPC)**.

social media specialists: Workers who plan, implement, and monitor a company's social media strategy and online reputation in order to increase brand awareness, improve marketing efforts, and increase overall sales. They create and administer content on social media platforms such as Facebook, Instagram, and Twitter to build an audience and encourage customer engagement.

user experience (UX) design: A design process that focuses on creating a user experience that is favorable and even leads users to certain conclusions, such as a buying point. By creating user interactions that are pleasant and desirable, the design becomes meaningful and relevant to users. UX design usually considers aspects of branding, design, usability, and function.

user interface design: The visual layout of the actual elements (such as buttons, icons, lists, and graphics) that users can interact with on a website or technological product. This often refers to the visual layout of a web page or smartphone screen.

web analytics specialists: Workers who determine the costs, benefits, and effectiveness of websites by gathering and interpreting data related to traffic to the site (such as how many visitors come to the site, which pages they visit, which areas they click, how long they stay, and so on). *See also* **Google Analytics**.

web app: An application that runs in a web browser, for example, webmail applications like Gmail, which stores your account data (your e-mail) in the Google cloud. You can access a web app from any computer connected to the internet using a standard browser. Web apps are typically platform/OS-independent since the website serves as the user interface.

web development: A broad term that refers to the varied tasks involved in creating a website or web application that will be hosted on the internet or on a local intranet. Web development includes designing the interface and the website; creating, programming, testing, and formatting the web content; client-side/server-side scripting for handling user interactions; managing and configuring network security; and more.

wireframe layout: A visual guide that shows the skeletal framework of a design piece, such as a website. Wireframes are created to help visualize and arrange elements before the details are added. For websites, wireframes usually show which elements will exist on which pages. This is different from a mock-up, which usually shows more visual details (such as colors, type used, and other elements).

Notes

Introduction

1. Bureau of Labor Statistics, US Department of Labor, "Public Relations Specialists: Summary," *Occupational Outlook Handbook*, https://www.bls.gov/ooh/media-and-communication/public-relations-specialists.htm.

2. Bureau of Labor Statistics, US Department of Labor, "Advertising, Promotions, and Marketing Managers," *Occupational Outlook Handbook*, https://www.bls.gov/ooh/management/advertising-promotions-and-marketing-managers.htm.

3. Bureau of Labor Statistics, US Department of Labor, "Market Research Analysts," *Occupational Outlook Handbook*, https://www.bls.gov/ooh/business-and-financial/market-research-analysts.htm.

4. Elka Torpey, "You're a *What?* Social Media Specialist," *Career Outlook*, November 2016, https://www.bls.gov/careeroutlook/2016/youre-a-what/social-media-specialist.htm.

5. Bureau of Labor Statistics, US Department of Labor, "Graphic Designers: Job Outlook," *Occupational Outlook Handbook*, https://www.bls.gov/ooh/arts-and-design/graphic-designers.htm#tab-6.

Chapter 1

1. Bureau of Labor Statistics, US Department of Labor, "Graphic Designers: How to Become a Graphic Designer," *Occupational Outlook Handbook*, https://www.bls.gov/ooh/arts-and-design/graphic-designers.htm#tab-4.

2. Workable.com, "Digital Media Specialist Job Description," https://resources.workable.com/digital-media-specialist-job-description.

3. CareerExplorer, "What Does a Digital Marketing Specialist Do?" https://www.careerexplorer.com/careers/digital-marketing-specialist/.

4. Elka Torpey, "You're a *What?* Social Media Specialist," *Career Outlook*, November 2016, https://www.bls.gov/careeroutlook/2016/youre-a-what/social-media-specialist.htm.

5. Chegg CareerMatch, "Web Analytics Specialist," https://www.careermatch.com/job-prep/career-insights/profiles/web-analytics-specialist/.

6. Wikipedia, "Graphic Design Occupations," https://en.wikipedia.org/wiki/Graphic_design_occupations.

7. Bureau of Labor Statistics, US Department of Labor, "Graphic Designers: Work Environment," *Occupational Outlook Handbook*, https: //www.bls.gov/ooh/arts-and-design/graphic-designers.htm#tab-3.

8. Monster.com, "Graphic Designer Job Description Sample," https://hiring.monster.com/employer-resources/job-description-templates/graphic-designer-job-description-sample/.

9. Ultimate Brand Bible, "What Does a Brand Manager Do, Day to Day?" https://ultimatebrandbible.com/what-does-a-brand-manager-do-day-to-day.

10. FlexJobs, "Product Marketing," https://www.flexjobs.com/blog/post/marketing-careers-types.

11. Campaign, "Job Description: Product Marketing Manager," https://www.campaignlive.co.uk/article/job-description-product-marketing-manager/1381297.

12. Bureau of Labor Statistics, US Department of Labor, "Web Developers and Digital Designers," *Occupational Outlook Handbook*, https://www.bls.gov/ooh/computer-and-information-technology/web-developers.htm.

13. Turpey, "Social Media Specialist."

14. Study.com, "SEO Specialist: Job Description, Salary & Training," *Occupational Outlook Handbook*, https://study.com/articles/seo_specialist_job_description_salary_training.html

15. Bureau of Labor Statistics, US Department of Labor, "Advertising, Promotions and Marketing Managers," *Occupational Outlook Handbook*, https://www.bls.gov/ooh/management/advertising-promotions-and-marketing-managers.htm.

16. Bureau of Labor Statistics, US Department of Labor, "Graphic Designers: Job Outlook," *Occupational Outlook Handbook*, https://www.bls.gov/ooh/arts-and-design/graphic-designers.htm#tab-6.

Chapter 2

1. *U.S. News & World Report*, "Marketing Manager," https://money.usnews.com /careers/best-jobs/marketing-manager.

2. Mathew Hilton, "Leverage Your Volunteering Experience," Eyes On Eyecare, May 11, 2016, https://eyesoneyecare.com/resources/volunteer-experience -physical-therapy-school/.

3. Lou Adler, "New Survey Reveals 85% of All Jobs Are Filled via Networking," LinkedIn, February 29, 2016, https: //www.linkedin.com/pulse/new-survey-reveals -85-all-jobs-filled-via-networking-lou-adler/.

Chapter 3

1. Gap Year Association, "Gap Year Data and Benefits," https://www.gapyearasso ciation.org/data-benefits.php.

2. Isaac Asimov, *The Roving Mind* (Amherst, NY: Prometheus Books, 1983), 116.

3. Peter Van Buskirk, "Finding a Good College Fit," *U.S. News & World Report*, June 13, 2011, https://www.usnews.com/education/blogs/the-college-admissions -insider/2011/06/13/finding-a-good-college-fit.

4. National Center for Education Statistics, "Fast Facts: Graduation Rates," https://nces.ed.gov/fastfacts/display.asp?id=40.

5. US Department of Education, "Focusing Higher Education on Student Success," July 27, 2015, https://nces.ed.gov/fastfacts/display.asp?id=40.

6. Department of Education, National Center for Education Statistics, "Table 502.30: Median Annual Earnings of Full-Time Year-Round Workers 25 to 34 Years Old and Full-Time Year-Round Workers as a Percentage of the Labor Force, by Sex, Race/ Ethnicity, and Educational Attainment: Selected Years, 1995 through 2013," *Digest for Education Statistics*, https://nces.ed.gov/programs/digest/d14/tables/dt14_502.30.asp.

7. Bureau of Labor Statistics. Current Population Survey. http: //www.bls.gov /cps/cpsaat07. htm

8. US Department of Education, "Six-Year Attainment, Persistence, Transfer, Retention, and Withdrawal Rates of Students Who Began Postsecondary Education in 2003–04," July 2011, https://nces.ed.gov/pubs2011/2011152.pdf.

9. Karen DeFelice, "Create an Awesome Design Portfolio with These 20 Pro Tips," Canva, https://www.canva.com/learn/portfolio/.

10. Allison Wignall, "Preference of the ACT or SAT by State (Infographic)," CollegeRaptor, November 14, 2019, https://www.collegeraptor.com/getting-in /articles/act-sat/preference-act-sat-state-infographic/.

11. College Board, "Focus on Net Price, Not Sticker Price," *BigFuture*, https://bigfuture.collegeboard.org/pay-for-college/paying-your-share/focus-on -net-price-not-sticker-price.

12. Jennifer Ma, Sandy Baum, Matea Pender, and C. J. Libassi. *Trends in College Pricing 2019* (New York: College Board, 2019), https://research.collegeboard.org /trends/college-pricing/highlights. Full report at https://research.collegeboard.org /trends/college-pricing/figures-tables/average-net-price-sector-over-time.

13. Federal Student Aid, "Learn What's New with the FAFSA Process," Financial Aid Toolkit, https://financialaidtoolkit.ed.gov/tk/learn/fafsa/updates.jsp.

14. Edith Hamilton, quoted in the *Saturday Evening Post*, September 27, 1958.

Chapter 4

1. Joshua Waldman, *Job Searching with Social Media for Dummies*, 2nd ed. (Hoboken, NJ: Wiley, 2013), 149.

2. Justin Ross Muchnick, *Teens' Guide to College & Career Planning*, 12th ed. (Lawrenceville, NJ: Peterson's, 2015), 179–80.

3. Mind Tools, "Active Listening: Hear What People Are Really Saying," https:// www.mindtools.com/CommSkll/ActiveListening.htm.

4. Career Builder, "Number of Employers Using Social Media to Screen Candidates Has Increased 500 Percent over the Last Decade," April 28, 2016, http://www.careerbuilder.com/share/aboutus/pressreleasesdetail.aspx?ed=12%2 F31%2F2016&id=pr945&sd=4%2F28%2F2016.

5. Alice E. M. Underwood, "9 Things to Avoid on Social Media While Looking for a New Job," Glassdoor, January 3, 2018, https://www.glassdoor.com/blog /things-to-avoid-on-social-media-job-search/.

Glossary

1. *Wikipedia*, "Search Engine Optimization," https://en.wikipedia.org/wiki /Search_engine_optimization.

Resources

If you are looking for more information about anything you read in this book, the resources gathered here can be a great jumping-off point. Try these resources as a starting point on your journey toward finding a great career!

Books

Fiske, Edward. *Fiske Guide to Colleges*. Naperville, IL: Sourcebooks, 2018.

Muchnick, Justin Ross. *Teens' Guide to College & Career Planning*, 12th ed. Lawrenceville, NJ: Peterson's, 2015.

Princeton Review. *The Best 382 Colleges, 2018 Edition: Everything You Need to Make the Right College Choice*. New York: Princeton Review, 2018.

Websites

American Gap Year Association
www.gapyearassociation.org
The American Gap Year Association's mission is "making transformative gap years an accessible option for all high school graduates." A gap year is a year taken between high school and college to travel, teach, work, volunteer, generally mature, and otherwise experience the world. Their website has lots of advice and resources for anyone considering taking a gap year.

American Indian College Fund
https://collegefund.org

This organization provides scholarships and college information for Native American students at any of the thirty-three accredited tribal colleges and universities in the United States.

American Marketing Association

www.ama.org

The tag line of the American Marketing Association is "your home for marketing career advice, trends and insights." The site includes information about jobs and training in your area, certifications, and trending news and the latest information related to marketing careers, and is a good place to make connections with other marketing professionals.

The Balance

www.thebalance.com

This site is all about managing money and finances, but also has a large section called Your Career, which provides advice for writing résumés and cover letters, interviewing, and more. Search the site for teens and you can find teen-specific advice and tips.

Cappex

www.cappex.com

Cappex is a free website where you can find out about colleges and merit aid scholarships.

The College Entrance Examination Board

www.collegeboard.org

The College Entrance Examination Board tracks and summarizes financial data from colleges and universities all over the United States. This great, well-organized site can be your one-stop shop for all things college research. It contains lots of advice and information about taking and doing well on the SAT and ACT, many articles on college planning, a robust college search feature, a scholarship search feature, and a major and career search area. You can type your career of interest (for example, digital advertising) into the search box and get back a full page that describes the career; gives advice on how to prepare, where to get experience, and how to pay for it; describes the characteristics you should have to excel in this career; lists helpful classes to take while in high school, and provides lots of links for more information.

College Grad Career Profiles
www.collegegrad.com/careers

Although this site is primarily geared toward college graduates, the careers profiles area, indicated above, has a list of links to nearly every career you could ever think of. A single click takes you to a very detailed, helpful section that describes the job in detail, explains the educational requirements, includes links to good colleges that offer this career and to actual open jobs and internships, describes the licensing requirements (if any), lists salaries, and much more.

Gates Millennium Scholars
https://gmsp.org

This organization provides scholarships to reduce barriers to college for African American, American Indian/Alaska Native, Asian Pacific Islander American, and Hispanic American students regardless of major.

GoCollege
www.gocollege.com

Calling itself the number one college-bound website on the internet, GoCollege provides lots of good tips and information about getting money and scholarships for college and getting the most out of your college education. This site also includes a good section on how scholarships in general work.

Go Overseas
www.gooverseas.com

Go Overseas claims to be your guide to more than fourteen thousand study and teach abroad programs that will change how you see the world. The site also includes information about high school abroad programs, and gap year opportunities, and includes community reviews and information about finding programs specific to your interests.

Khan Academy

www.khanacademy.org

The Khan Academy website is an impressive collection of articles, courses, and
videos about many educational topics in math, science, and the human-
ities. You can search any topic or subject (by subject matter and grade), and
read lessons, take courses, and watch videos to learn all about it. The site
includes test prep information for the SAT, ACT, AP, GMAT, and other
standardized tests. There is also a College Admissions tab with lots of good
articles and information, provided in the approachable Khan style.

Live Career Website

www.livecareer.com

This site has an impressive number of resources directed toward teens for
writing résumés and cover letters, as well as interviewing.

Mapping Your Future

www.mappingyourfuture.org

This site helps young people figure out what they want to do and maps out how
to reach career goals. Includes helpful tips on résumé writing, job hunting,
job interviewing, and more.

Monster.com

www.monster.com

Monster.com is perhaps the most well-known and certainly one of the largest
employment websites in the United States. You fill in a couple of search
boxes and away you go. You can sort by job title, of course, as well as by
company name, location, salary range, experience range, and much more.
The site also includes information about career fairs, advice on résumés and
interviewing, and more.

Occupational Outlook Handbook

www.bls.gov/ooh

The US Bureau of Labor Statistics produces this website, which offers lots of
relevant and updated information about various careers, including average
salaries, how to work in the industry, the job market outlook, typical work

environments, and what workers do on the job. See www.bls.gov/emp/ for a full list of employment projections.

Peterson's College Prep
www.petersons.com
In addition to lots of information about preparing for the ACT and SAT and easily searchable information about scholarships nationwide, the Peterson's site includes a comprehensive search feature for universities and schools based on location, major, name, and more.

Study.com
www.study.com
Similar to Khan Academy, Study.com allows you to search any topic or subject and read lessons, take courses, and watch videos to learn all about it. The site includes a good collection of information about the digital communications professions.

TeenLife: College Preparation
www.teenlife.com
This site calls itself "the leading source for college preparation" and includes lots of information about summer programs, gap year programs, community service, and more. Promoting the belief that spending time out "in the world" outside of the classroom can help students develop important life skills, this site contains lots of links to volunteer and summer programs.

U.S. News & World Report College Rankings
www.usnews.com/best-colleges
U.S. News & World Report provides almost fifty different types of numerical rankings and lists of colleges throughout the United States to help students with their college search. You can search colleges by best reviewed, best value for the money, best liberal arts schools, best schools for B students, and more.

Bibliography

Adler, Lou. "New Survey Reveals 85% of All Jobs Are Filled Via Networking." LinkedIn, February 29, 2016. Retrieved April 30, 2021, from https://www.linkedin.com/pulse/new-survey-reveals-85-all-jobs-filled-via-networking-lou-adler/.

Asimov, Isaac. *The Roving Mind.* Amherst, NY: Prometheus Books, 1983.

Balance.com. "Career Choices." April 24, 2018. Retrieved January 10, 2021, from https://www.thebalance.com/career-choice-or-change-4161891.

Boyle, Justin. "How Much Does Trade School Cost?" Real Work Matters, September 10, 2019. Retrieved February 19, 2021, https://www.rwm.org/articles/how-much-does-trade-school-cost/.

Bureau of Labor Statistics, US Department of Labor. Healthcare Occupations. www.bls.gov/ooh/healthcare.

———. "Advertising, Promotions, and Marketing Managers." *Occupational Outlook Handbook.* https://www.bls.gov/ooh/management/advertising-promotions-and-marketing-managers.htm.

———. "Graphic Designers: How to Become a Graphic Designer." *Occupational Outlook Handbook.* https: //www.bls.gov/ooh/arts-and-design/graphic-designers.htm#tab-4.

———. "Graphic Designers: Job Outlook." *Occupational Outlook Handbook.* https://www.bls.gov/ooh/arts-and-design/graphic-designers.htm#tab-6.

———. "Graphic Designers: Work Environment." *Occupational Outlook Handbook.* https: //www.bls.gov/ooh/arts-and-design/graphic-designers.htm#tab-3.

———. "Market Research Analysts." *Occupational Outlook Handbook.* https://www.bls.gov/ooh/business-and-financial/market-research-analysts.htm.

———. "Public Relations Specialists: Summary." *Occupational Outlook Handbook.* https://www.bls.gov/ooh/media-and-communication/public-relations-specialists.htm.

———. "Web Developers and Digital Designers." *Occupational Outlook Handbook*. https://www.bls.gov/ooh/computer-and-information-techno logy/web-developers.htm.

Campaign. "Job Description: Product Marketing Manager." https://www.campaignlive.co.uk/article/job-description-product-marketing-manager/1381297.

Career Builder. "Number of Employers Using Social Media to Screen Candidates Has Increased 500 Percent over the Last Decade." April 28, 2016. http://www.careerbuilder.com/share/aboutus/pressreleasesdetail.aspx ?ed=12%2F31%2F2016&id=pr945&sd=4%2F28%2F2016.

CareerBuilder.com. Press releases. Retrieved March 9, 2021, from http:// www.careerbuilder.com/share/aboutus/pressreleasesdetail.aspx?ed =12%2F31%2F2016&id=pr945&sd=4%2F28%2F2016.

CareerExplorer. "What Does a Digital Marketing Specialist Do?" https://www .careerexplorer.com/careers/digital-marketing-specialist/.

Chegg CareerMatch. "Web Analytics Specialist." https://www.careermatch .com/job-prep/career-insights/profiles/web-analytics-specialist/.

College Board. "Focus on Net Price, Not Sticker Price." *BigFuture*. https:// bigfuture.collegeboard.org/pay-for-college/paying-your-share/focus -on-net-price-not-sticker-price.

College Entrance Examination Board. "Understanding College Costs." Retrieved March 18, 2021, from https://bigfuture.collegeboard.org /pay-for-college/college-costs/understanding-college-costs.

Common Core State Standards Initiative. http://www.corestandards.org.

DeFelice, Karen. "Create an Awesome Design Portfolio with These 20 Pro Tips." Canva. https://www.canva.com/learn/portfolio/.

Department of Education, National Center for Education Statistics. "Table 502.30: Median Annual Earnings of Full-Time Year-Round Workers 25 to 34 Years Old and Full-Time Year-Round Workers as a Percentage of the Labor Force, by Sex, Race/Ethnicity, and Educational Attainment: Selected Years, 1995 through 2013." *Digest for Education Statistics*. https:// nces.ed.gov/programs/digest/d14/tables/dt14_502.30.asp.

Federal Student Aid. "Learn What's New with the FAFSA Process." Financial Aid Toolkit. Retrieved March 29, 2021, from https://financialaidtoolkit .ed.gov/tk/learn/fafsa/updates.jsp.

Fiske, Edward. *Fiske Guide to Colleges*. Naperville, IL: Sourcebooks, 2018.

FlexJobs. "Product Marketing," Retrieved April 27, 2021, from https://www .flexjobs.com/blog/post/marketing-careers-types.

Gap Year Association. "Gap Year Data and Benefits." https://www.gapyearasso ciation.org/data-benefits.php.

———. "Research Statement." Retrieved April 18, 2021, from https://gap yearassociation.org/about.php/.

GoCollege. "Types of Scholarships." Retrieved April 25, 2021, from http:// www.gocollege.com/financial-aid/scholarships/types/.

Hamilton, Edith. Quoted in the *Saturday Evening Post*. September 27, 1958.

Hilton, Mathew. "Leverage Your Volunteering Experience." Eyes On Eyecare. May 11, 2016. https://eyesoneyecare.com/resources/volunteer-experience -physical-therapy-school/.

Keates, Cathy. "What Is Job Shadowing?" *TalentEgg*. Retrieved April 25, 2021, from https://talentegg.ca/incubator/2011/02/03/what-is-job-shadowing / [article discontinued].

Ladders. "Eye-Tracking Study." Retrieved April 30, 2021, https://cdn.the ladders.net/static/images/basicSite/pdfs/TheLadders-EyeTracking -StudyC2.pdf.

Ma, Jennifer, Sandy Baum, Matea Pender, and C. J. Libassi. *Trends in College Pricing 2019*. New York: College Board, 2019.

Mind Tools. "Active Listening: Hear What People Are Really Saying." Retrieved April 10, 2021, from https://www.mindtools.com/CommSkll /ActiveListening.htm.

Monster.com. "Graphic Designer Job Description Sample." Retrieved April 18, 2021, from https://hiring.monster.com/employer-resources/job -description-templates/graphic-designer-job-description-sample/.

Muchnick, Justin Ross. *Teens' Guide to College & Career Planning*, 12th ed. Lawrenceville, NJ: Peterson's, 2015.

National Center for Education Statistics. "Fast Facts: Graduation Rates." Retrieved February 10, 2021, from https://nces.ed.gov/fastfacts/display .asp?id=40.

Ryan, Liz. "12 Qualities Employers Look for When They're Hiring." *Forbes*, March 2, 2016. Retrieved April 15, 2021, from https://www.forbes.com /sites/lizryan/2016/03/02/12-qualities-employers-look-for-when-theyre -hiring/#8ba06d22c242.

Study.com. "SEO Specialist: Job Description, Salary & Training." *Occupational Outlook Handbook.* https://study.com/articles/seo_specialist_job_descrip tion_salary_training.html.

Torpey, Elka. "You're a *What*? Social Media Specialist." *Career Outlook.* November 2016, https://www.bls.gov/careeroutlook/2016/youre-a-what /social-media-specialist.htm.

Ultimate Brand Bible. "What Does a Brand Manager Do, Day to Day?" https:// ultimatebrandbible.com/what-does-a-brand-manager-do-day-to-day.

Underwood, Alice E. M. "9 Things to Avoid on Social Media While Looking for a New Job." Glassdoor, January 3, 2018. https://www.glassdoor.com /blog/things-to-avoid-on-social-media-job-search/.

US Department of Education. "Focusing Higher Education on Student Success." July 27, 2015. Retrieved February 18, 2021, from https://www .ed.gov/news/press-releases/fact-sheet-focusing-higher-education-stu dent-success [article discontinued].

———. "Six-Year Attainment, Persistence, Transfer, Retention, and Withdrawal Rates of Students Who Began Postsecondary Education in 2003–04." July 2011. https://nces.ed.gov/pubs2011/2011152.pdf.

U.S. News & World Report. "Marketing Manager." https://money.usnews.com /careers/best-jobs/marketing-manager.

Van Buskirk, Peter. "Finding a Good College Fit." *U.S. News & World Report*, June 13, 2011. Retrieved April 18, 2021, from https://www.us news.com/education/blogs/the-college-admissions-insider/2011/06/13 /finding-a-good-college-fit.

Waldman, Joshua. *Job Searching with Social Media for Dummies*, 2nd ed. Hoboken, NJ: Wiley, 2013.

Wignall, Allison. "Preference of the ACT or SAT by State (Infographic)." CollegeRaptor, November 14, 2019. https://www.collegeraptor.com /getting-in/articles/act-sat/preference-act-sat-state-infographic/.

Wikipedia. "Graphic Design Occupations." https://en.wikipedia.org/wiki /Graphic_design_occupations.

Workable.com. "Digital Media Specialist Job Description." https://resources .workable.com/digital-media-specialist-job-description.

About the Author

Kezia Endsley is an editor and author from Indianapolis, Indiana. In addition to editing technical publications and writing books for teens, she enjoys running and triathlons, traveling, reading, and spending time with her family and many pets.